— *The* —
WILLIAM MARVY
COMPANY *of St. Paul*

• *Keeping Barbershops Classic* •

CURT BROWN

Foreword by ERIC DREGNI

THE
History
PRESS

Published by The History Press
Charleston, SC 29403
www.historypress.net

Copyright © 2015 by Curt Brown
All rights reserved

Front cover: Photograph by Annie Griffiths and reprinted with permission
of the National Geographic Society.

First published 2015

Manufactured in the United States

ISBN 978.1.62619.569.1

Library of Congress Control Number: 2014953430

CONTENTS

FOREWORD

How many times did I drive by the Marvy Company on St. Clair Avenue in St. Paul and not realize what history hid behind those doors? The brick building is an old auto repair shop and seemed like an odd place for a barbershop. I thought even the name "Marvy" was a trumped-up synonym for "marvelous" rather than the real name of William Marvy, who founded the shop to sell the last barber poles in the country. Only when I dared enter did I learn a bit of the history that Curt Brown has uncovered in-depth with his research for this book.

Inside, I learned how the haircutting biz has been cleaned up from the days when barbers doubled as doctors to lance boils, yank teeth and even bleed patients with leeches. The rags to sop up the extra blood were hung outside to dry. As the cloths spun into a spiral in the wind, they served as an advertisement for the services offered inside—even better than the ditty "shave and a haircut…two bits." Marvy's modern barber poles cleaned up this image and saved it from oblivion by making it "six ways better" than the passé poles of yore.

So sit back and enjoy the story about the preservation of this great symbol of the barber pole that stems back to medieval times.

ERIC DREGNI
Author of *In Cod We Trust: Living the Norwegian Dream, Minnesota Marvels: Roadside Attractions in the Land of Lakes* and seven other books

ACKNOWLEDGMENTS

I first walked into the William Marvy Company's brick vortex in St. Paul in 1997, reporting on a business story for the *Minneapolis Star Tribune*. Sadly, William had passed away four years earlier.

But his son Robert and grandsons Scott and Dan have been kind enough to trust me with their methodically preserved family archives: from William Marvy's teenage diaries to the company's ledger books and the secrets cradled on every line. Their cooperation was instrumental in telling their patriarch's story, as was Rimon, the Minnesota Jewish Arts Council. The arts-supporting panel of the Minneapolis Jewish Federation helped this Jewish writer expand his chops and share a quintessential tale of Minnesota Jewish chutzpah.

I'm also indebted to Marvy barber pole makers Scott Gohr and Chue Vang; fellow chronicler of the offbeat tale Eric Dregni; Macalester College professor of history Dr. Norm Rosenberg, who lent me his copy of Mic Hunter's delightful *The American Barbershop: A Closer Look at a Disappearing Place*; Donald Katz's peerless history on the second half of the twentieth century, *Home Fires*; research aides and dear friends Richard Fohrman, Bill McAuliffe, David Reitan and Bill Sands; Howard Warner, executive director of the Ohio Barbers Board, who created the Barber Hall of Fame's online biographies; Barber Car maker Joe Bailon and his great-nephew Ray Olivas; the National Barber Hall of Fame Kirkpatricks, Ken Kirkpatrick in Minnesota and Charles Kirkpatrick in Arkansas; and their countless fellow barbers from Boston to Los Angeles who visited with a curious writer who became an obsessive barber pole chaser: Jim Stroh in Tomah, Wisconsin; Ray Opatz in St. Cloud, Minnesota; Robert Layne and Leroy Young in Chicago; Gilbert Peppin in St. Paul; Peggy Schmidt and Kelly Sharp in Minneapolis; Aneury J. Brito near Boston; Carlos Jimenez near Los Angeles; Rob Petrie in Telluride and Merv Bergal and Amador Tucson in Durango, Colorado; father and son Clyde and Mark Schafer near Tampa and Toledo, respectively; Brian Franke in New Hope, Minnesota; Barber Hall of Fame director Mike Ippoliti near Columbus, Ohio; and the irrepressible immigrant from Hartford, Connecticut, via Minnesota and Kosovo, Nazim (Noli) Salihu. Finally, special shout-outs go to Anita Duquette at the Whitney Museum; Greg Dumais and Julia Turner at The History Press; my daughter, Mackenzie, for searching for serial numbers in California; and my wife, Adele, for joining me on this quirky journey.

Introduction

You went up a long lane through groves to find it. When you stepped out and walked through the door, your short article turned into a book.
—John McPhee, Oranges, *1966*

I descend rickety wooden stairs—more like a haphazard cascade of weathered boards held together with a few rusty nails. There are no handrails.

The basement is dark and has a dirt floor. Brick pavers and limestone jut out from mud walls as they have since the 1880s.

So many brick chunks have loosened and fallen that there's a pile in front of me as I step off the last plank of stairs. I gingerly tiptoe around them and illuminate the darkness with my cellphone's greenish glow.

According to Jim Stroh, whose barbershop is bustling above in Tomah, Wisconsin, the ladder should be at the bottom of the stairs. It's not.

The darkness eases as my eyes adjust. I see a bent, aluminum ladder at the basement's far end. I inch ahead amid fallen rock, sure a rat will crawl up my pant leg any second. I grab the ladder, balancing it precariously as I make my way up the stairs and into the Saturday morning swirl of Stroh's Barbershop.

A couple of old-timers wait, watching an outdoors hunting show on a TV mounted high on the wall beside stuffed deer heads. A father, his five-year-old son perched on his lap, chats as Jim cuts the kid's bangs.

They all look at me quizzically as I weave through the shop, dodging mirrors and patrons before waltzing my way out the front door.

I plant the ladder next to the entrance of Stroh's Barbershop on the corner of Superior Avenue and Monowa Street, in the heart of downtown

Tomah—if not the heart of America. The surrounding storefronts include the Crow Bar, Teepee Supper Club, High Guns and Firearms, Egstad Insurance & Inspection, Marilyn's School of Dance, Amish Country Corner, a variety store and a tattoo parlor.

I climb four steps up the ladder until I'm face-to-face with the two-pronged target of this quixotic journey. The doorway into Stroh's Barbershop is framed by not one but two Marvy Model 55 barber poles. Like the other eighty-five thousand Marvy barber poles made since 1950, these two aluminum and stainless steel iconic symbols feature rounded and reflective bowls up top and on the bottom that serve as caps and bases for the tubular glass cylinders housing the swirling red, white and blue diagonally spinning stripes.

The Marvy barber pole is a nostalgic survivor, still made by hand in a nondescript brick factory in St. Paul, Minnesota—creations of one of those quirky family businesses that started in the middle of the last century and today finds itself in a club of endangered species like the Javan rhinoceros and the ivory-billed woodpecker.

The William Marvy Company is the last manufacturer of barber poles in the Americas—north, central and south. Japan, China and Europe continue to crank out a few poles. But Marvy remains the king. Odds are, if you catch a glimpse of a barber pole on Main Streets in small-town America or in the heart of its big cities, it's a Marvy.

A half dozen companies from Detroit to San Francisco once made barber poles. Then the Beatles and the Vietnam War struck, hair grew long, barbershops shuttered and barber supply companies went belly-up—leaving only the William Marvy Company to extend the lifeline of a universal beacon that dates back to the Middle Ages, when barbers were surgeons. They pulled teeth, used leeches to suck diseased blood from patients and hung their bloody rags to dry in the wind, swirling red and white.

The late William Marvy, the storytelling, cigar-chomping entrepreneur whose creations still punctuate street corners across the globe, had a favorite yarn.

A northern Minnesota fisherman purchased a Marvy Model 55 barber pole to put at the end of his dock, a glowing guide to help him find his way home after a night of fishing. He returned the pole a week later, asking for a refund.

"What happened?" Marvy asked. "Why the change of heart?"

The man explained that he had a line of boats puttering up to his dock, their captains looking for haircuts.

Jim Stroh, at his barbershop in Tomah, Wisconsin, stands below one of his two Marvy poles—this one, No. 40,561, dates back to February 18, 1965, according to the red logbooks in the Marvy Company vault. *Photo by Curt Brown.*

"There isn't a more iconic symbol," Jim Stroh said between scissors snips in Tomah.

Jim is fifty, built like a bank vault, squat with hardly any hair atop his bullet-shaped head. He wore a teal barber's smock made of a shiny, synthetic fabric over a black T-shirt.

I explained to him how I had been commissioned to write a book about the William Marvy Company. A South Carolina publisher, The History Press, had seen a business feature story I wrote as a reporter for the *Minneapolis Star Tribune* back in 1997. It was intrigued by this last survivor of commerce, the lone barber pole maker left.

Jim Stroh, though, was too busy this springtime Saturday morning to really care. But he let me wander down to his basement and retrieve the old ladder I came to stand on.

Jim danced inside the window, his electric razor cleaning the nape of a customer's neck. I fished my reading glasses out of my pants' pocket, delicately maintaining my balance on the twisted ladder leaning against the weathered storefront.

It would be the first of countless such ladder ascents and visits to barbershops from Pasadena to Boston. I've often wondered what passersby thought I was doing, up on a ladder or stray chair, examining the fine print of a barber pole.

I spat on my fingertips and rubbed the grime and soot off the steel plate bearing the serial number of this Marvy Model 55. The one on the right side of the door is No. 8,945. The one on the left is the younger No. 40,561.

A few days later at the William Marvy Company offices, 165 miles west in St. Paul, the third-generation scion of this odd niche business let me into the vault. Dan Marvy plucked one of the blood-red logbooks off a shelf. His grandfather Bill—or, more accurately, his secretaries over the years—started keeping track of each and every Marvy pole. They noted the date it was created and which dealer took it to sell and install at barbershops from the Midwest to the Middle East. The company recently shipped some to Dubai through its network of global distributors.

Checking the ledger books, we learned that the one gracing the left side of Jim Stroh's door dates back to February 18, 1965—when someone employed by the Varna Barber Supply Company in Winona, Minnesota, filled his order. The older one on the right, No. 8,954, was built on the third day of 1956, at the height of the Eisenhower years—an era of abundance in America. The cold war with the Soviets was simmering, if that was even possible. Fathers took sons to get their hair cut, and a barber supply salesman from Kennedy's Barber Supply in Grand Rapids, Michigan, bought No. 8,945 and sold it in the middle of Wisconsin.

That's precisely how William Marvy spent the Great Depression: driving a panel truck around southwestern Minnesota in his twenties, selling clippers and hair tonic. Bill would spend weekdays on the road, returning on Friday night for Sabbath dinner at his in-laws'. If a barber wanted to add a new pole to his order, Bill, his dealer, would have to install the hundred-pound cast-iron and porcelain behemoth.

So when World War II ended in the 1940s and aluminum became available, Bill Marvy got an idea. He would make a modern, shiny barber

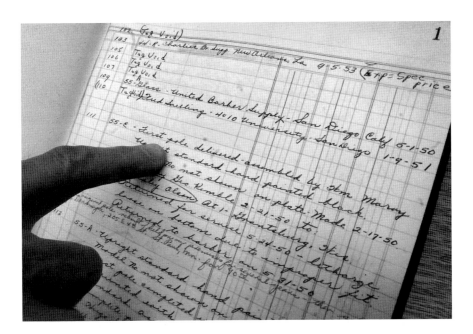

In one of dozens of logbooks in the company vault, William Marvy noted his first pole, made on February 17, 1950; installed four days later in Grantsburg, Wisconsin; and repaired three months after that. *Photo by John Doman.*

pole—lighter and shatterproof to ease barbers' concerns about vandalism. It would be electric. No more wind-up keys used to keep older barber poles spinning through their clock-like winding mechanisms.

Nearly eighty years and eighty-five thousand barber poles later, Marvy Model 55s and their larger and smaller cousins shine on main streets from Paris to, well, Tomah.

I collapse the ladder and return it to Jim Stroh's basement. Back in the shop, where stuffed birds join more than a dozen taxidermy mounts, World War II uniforms hang from the walls. One came from Lester Harris, an older customer with no kids to whom to bequeath his old uniform. The other came from an attic of a fellow barber. No one knows who once wore it. Jim explains how he went to a now-defunct barber school in La Crosse, Wisconsin, when his construction job dried up. He opened this shop on August 17, 2003.

"It's a dying business," he said. "Nothing to get into for the money."

But he loves the people and the banter. "And," the old-timer in his chair said with a chuckle, "you have a captive audience."

For years, that captive audience sat in the chair of Sheldon (Spike) Reavis, whose death in Tomah in 2003 spelled the end of Spike's Barbershop and opened the door for Stroh's Barbershop. Spike likely purchased the Marvy poles that hang outside. Then again, the customers and barbers caution, it might have been Paul Melby, another retired barber in town.

"There used to be six barbershops in Tomah with eleven barbers in 1951," Jim Stroh said. "Now I'm the only one. We're a dying breed."

The conversation bounces around until talk turns to what male bastions barbershops remain—"the only place left where you can tell women to leave the seat up," Jim said. "This is a guy place." And it's an old guy's place at that. Stroh's average customer is seventy. A dad comes in with two sons, ages fourteen and eleven. Stroh said they are among only about a dozen customers he has younger than eighteen.

"It's a changing culture in America," the old-timer in the chair said, as Jim works his razor and brush, sculpting a crew cut. "Half the marriages end in divorce, and kids are living with single moms, and they don't come to barbershops because dad isn't around."

Jim Stroh remembers when his mom took him to her "beauty parlor" for a perm in 1982.

"It was such a nightmare," he said. "I can still see the shop."

Everyone laughs, and I walk out the door and into the spring Wisconsin sunshine—between the twin sentinels of swirling red, white and blue Marvy barber poles.

1

EMERGING FROM THE BASEMENT

Before the Kennedys, before the Beatles
Before the Vietnam War
Back to a time when anything was possible
Having less meant knowing more.
—*Julie Gold, "Goodnight, New York."*

On New Year's Day 1950, at the midpoint of the twentieth century, forty-year-old William Marvy climbed the basement stairs at his family's home in St. Paul, Minnesota, a few blocks from the Mississippi River—the channel marking the symbolic middle of the nation.

Marvy was joined by his neighbor, Bill Harris, an electrical engineer and the father of another Jewish family who had started to populate the Highland Park area some five miles west of the neighborhoods skirting downtown St. Paul, where their parents lived.

Bill Marvy had paid Harris a few bucks for his expertise and purchased enough equipment and tools to forge a small machine shop in the basement at 446 Mount Curve Boulevard near the corner of Randolph and Cretin Avenues.

For countless nights spanning nearly all of 1949, the pair had disappeared into the basement to tinker in the makeshift shop. Marvy had collected sample parts of just about every type of barber pole ever made. Now it was time to figure out how to improve what had been tried for decades—centuries, really.

They experimented for months before electing to go with stainless steel and anodized aluminum. They settled on a striped swatch of red, white and blue plastic inside the cylinder, instead of the old paper ones that faded in the frigid Minnesota conditions. Using Lucite, a plexiglass alternative to real glass, would protect the pole from shattering. A chromium stainless steel standard backbone was rigged with four concave facets that gave the reflective impression of three spinning poles. And the first pole weighed so much less than its porcelain and cast-iron predecessors that Marvy no doubt grinned with satisfaction from the lightness of the creation he carried up the stairs that first day of 1950.

When he surfaced, red-eyed but smiling, Marvy cradled a contraption in his arms like a baby. It was the prototype of the Marvy Model 55. He plugged it in and invited his two sons, five-year-old Jim and not-quite-two Bob, to flip the switch.

With a whir, the red, white and blue cylinder began to spin. And the faces of the jubilant Marvy family reflected off the shiny stainless steel bowl that cupped the pole's lower end—a bowl that historians trace back to the leech containers that barber-surgeons used for bloodletting centuries ago as a universal cure-all method.

Neighbors likely heard no hollering or hoots of celebration from the Marvy home. It was a ten-degree day. Temperatures would drop to twenty-four degrees below zero in the coming weeks. The windows were shut tight. But the house was bathed with the kind of warmth that radiates from a tightknit family like the Marvys.

Not that everything was warm and cozy—a cranky mother, not fate, landed Bill Marvy in the basement of his handsome two-story house at 446 Mount Curve Boulevard with its ornate front-door vestibule that gave it an almost Moroccan flair. The house builder was Bill's father, a Latvian émigré and Jewish carpenter named Mair Mairovitz.

Born in 1874, Mair had sailed to America in 1902, been ushered through Ellis Island and gone to work in New York City. But his fear of heights made work hard to find in a city bursting with early skyscraper construction.

Someone told Mair to go to Minnesota, where the buildings weren't too tall and where he had some relatives. He had built houses and maintained properties for decades, including the stately and solid house on Mount Curve.

But Mair's wife, Molly, refused to live there because it was too far out—five miles from their Victorian house at 186 McBoal Street in the Upper Landing neighborhood where Jews, Italians, Swedes and Norwegians grew tomatoes together on the banks of the Mississippi. Mair and Molly were both born in Old World towns where they could walk to the butcher and everyone they knew lived nearby. She wasn't about to move out to the riverbank meadows of Highland Park.

So William Marvy moved into the house his father built and his mother rejected, along with his wife, Rose (née Goldberg), and their two young boys. A third son, their eldest, had died at age five of sudden pneumonia in 1946. Robert, the youngest, who would eventually take over the barber pole–manufacturing mantle from his father, was born in 1948 and was busy toddling around in diapers when that first pole came up from the basement on January 1, 1950.

Like their fellow post–World War II Americans, Bill and Rose Marvy were being not only productive citizens but also reproductive ones.

U.S. birth rates vaulted by nearly 20 percent from 1945 to 1946, spiking another 12 percent in 1947. A new American was boosting the nation's population every dozen seconds.

Most of the employed men in the country, back from World War II, were union members, and strikes erupted among steelworkers, autoworkers, coal miners, meat processors and telephone and electrical workers. They had fought hard and wanted their fair share of the burgeoning economic pie.

Bill Marvy, in that sense, was a rarity—one of roughly 15 percent of Americans who owned their own businesses in 1949 and the tools needed to perform their jobs. That number had flip-flopped in a century from the 85 percent of workers who owned their means of production in the mid-1800s.

Americans were literally buzzing in postwar euphoria, with half the electricity ever generated flowing through U.S. wires in the late 1940s. Half the world's electricity was serving 6 percent of the globe's population in the United States. Americans were told that they would soon cook dinner with the flip of a switch and live in plastic houses that could be delivered and constructed in hours.

The son of parents who never owned a car, Bill Marvy jumped on that modernization bandwagon and rode it with the flair of a carnival barker. A natural salesman, Marvy had started peddling newspapers before he turned ten years old. In later years, he often recalled sharp memories of selling newspapers on November 11, 1918—Armistice Day, when World War I ended.

"My mother never said to me as a boy, 'Come home after school, it's too cold to sell papers today,'" he once said. "What she did was make sure I was wearing my scarf and I would bring home twenty cents, maybe a quarter."

The fifth of six kids—three girls and then three boys—Bill Mairovitz (as he was known until 1935) gave up his newspaper hawking at age twelve. He found work after school and on Saturdays at a shoe repair shop that catered to government surplus, buying and fixing army boots from the Great War. Then he worked for a man who owned a furniture store.

By the time he turned thirteen, the Jewish year of the bar mitzvah rite of passage signaling manhood, Bill got a tip from his elder sister Florence. She worked as a bookkeeper for Western Barber Supply Company and got him in the door.

The boss told him he could fold and mail circulars after school and on Saturdays. Though it sounds boring for a young teenager, for the first time, Bill had what he called a formal job. He was paid by check after receiving cash at his newspaper, shoe repair and furniture store gigs. Work slowly began to dominate his days, which was and always would be fine with William Marvy.

He received permission from the administration at his school—now-defunct Mechanic Arts High School—to get out at noon everyday because his boss needed him at Western Barber Supply. The wholesaler dealt in a wide collection of barber, beauty and drugstore goods.

The job gave Bill confidence and some bragging rights. His boss often gave him a car to get to work, making him the only kid who drove to school. He could leave work at six o'clock at night and be home for dinner seven minutes later.

During Bill's childhood, the Mairovitzes lived at 186 McBoal Street, at the corner with Leech Street in the old melting pot of Jews and Italians in St. Paul's Upper Landing neighborhood. They were mostly working-class wage earners in the tightknit neighborhood, with a few shopkeepers and professionals sprinkled in.

The house stood a few blocks from the High Bridge that spanned the Mississippi River gorge. More importantly for young Bill Mairovitz, they were within a mile of downtown St. Paul. He would walk downtown or spend a nickel for a streetcar ride to get to the pool halls, movie palaces and business hubbub. When he got the keys to the car from work, he would round up his buddies every night after dinner and cruise down to their favorite Wabasha Street pool hall for some snooker.

When America plunged into the Great Depression, the Mairovitzes hardly felt it at first. Bill was twenty and had been working for more than ten years. He always had money in his pocket. And his carpenter father had built enough new homes to rent out properties and avoid feeling the pinch. By the mid-1930s, that would change.

At Western Supply, young William Mairovitz had gradually climbed the ladder, going from floor sweeping to operating the mimeograph machine, addressing fliers, running errands and stirring up so much lilac water that people would avoid sitting near him on his trolley rides home. He earned $3.50 a week, working five days after school and on Saturdays. While his Old World parents kept kosher and observed the Sabbath, Bill was among a generation of American Jews shucking off those ancient rituals and observances to fit more seamlessly into a modern world.

The young Mairovitz was also an ardent journal keeper. He would chronicle his teenage years in a thin gray diary with red tape reinforcing its spine. The book was called the Educator, Student-Sized Note Book, No. 308. On its cover, makers had imprinted a drawing of an oil lamp like Aladdin's sitting on a stack of books with a globe hovering in the background.

On February 8, 1926, when he was sixteen, Bill Marvy glued in his diary a small black-and-white photograph of himself—squarish jaw, cleft chin and straight-ahead eyes exuding confidence atop a skinny black tie and too-tight sports jacket.

The diary entries don't reveal much. But they list the comings and goings of a kid in the 1920s: following his "Pa" to house repair jobs, playing snooker and tennis, going dancing at this and that club and attending the since-shuttered Mechanic Arts High

Glued into one of his journals is a photo of William Marvy in 1926, when he was sixteen. *Photo by Curt Brown.*

A young William Marvy kept journals in the 1920s, detailing when he practiced his saxophone, played snooker, studied schoolwork, went dancing and retired for the night. *Photo by Curt Brown.*

School in St. Paul before he dropped out at age sixteen to work full time. "April 1, 1925: School, work, practice on sax. April 5: Clean and repaired gas stove, practice on sax, take a walk in the evening. Retire 10 pm. April 8: Work, walk, played pool, sax lesson, practice. Retire 11 pm. April 22: Painted screen porch. Got a sports blouse at Shapiro's ($2.45), got shoes shined, went to operetta at Mechanics Arts High, Robin Hood. Retired at midnight."

By May 1925, he was ordering barber supplies, soliciting orders and visiting barbershops. If he loved what he was doing, he didn't say. The journals are thin of emotion but include a few tales of love requited, like one on September 21, 1929: "…We did a little loving…but I told her to try to forget me…by then her eyes became wet with tears that began to drop like water out of a faucet."

Such juicy entries were rare. It was more typical for Marvy to make a mention that he "attended barber supply dealers dinner and meeting at the Radisson Hotel. Started at 6 lasted til 11. New discounts were discussed" or that on June 1, 1925, he "went to Stillwater with Bunny and Joe. Didn't get any orders. Shined shoes, went to the Coliseum (dance hall). Retired at 1:15 a.m. Slept in the front room."

He did account for all his purchases, from saxophone reeds ("two for 50 cents") to "light gray spring trousers at Herman and Clark's for $5" and "a sports sweater at Broadwins for $2.65."

He noted seeing President Calvin Coolidge at an industrial parade on June 8, 1925, and "helping some black folks out of a ditch with their car" on a trek to Duluth on Independence Day 1925 that included stops in the Iron Range town of Hibbing.

Bill had one foot in the adult world of sales but was still a sixteen-year-old kid. On February 2, 1926, he "bet Mr. Duetsch I could eat 14 Coney Island sandwiches in less than 40 minutes. I won the bet by eating 14 sandwiches in 22 minutes."

As the 1920s rolled on, there were more entries about barber conventions and visits to barber supply companies. He seldom discussed his religious faith, except one night in April 1928, when he listened with a friend to a political debate on the radio. The debate centered on whether Jews should vote automatically for Jewish candidates.

"Pa was on the affirmative. I stood on the negative. They say give a Jew a chance to get started. I say bar race and religion from politics. Vote for a man on his merits. I would just as soon associate with Negros as white people. The reason why I don't is because it would appear very conspicuous."

Such questions of race and religious identity proved to be more than debate fodder for the young Mairovitz.

While German Jews had been in St. Paul since before Minnesota's statehood in 1858, and Russian and Eastern European Jews fleeing the pogroms around 1900 added to their numbers, Minnesota Jews were still a tiny minority. And anti-Semitism seeped into a place known for its niceness. Jews had opened their own hospital, Mount Sinai, when Jewish doctors were denied access to other medical facilities. Summer resorts on Lake Minnetonka advertised that they catered to "Gentiles Only."

Neighborhood restrictions that barred Jews, blacks and Italians were commonplace.

When one of the Mairovitz cousins tried to page a family member at Newman's Department Store in the mid-1930s in downtown St. Paul, the clerk refused—saying they wouldn't be paging anyone named Mairovitz. The reason was easy enough to grasp.

So one day in 1935, the whole clan headed to the Ramsey County courthouse. And with a judge's approval and signature, the Mairovitzes became the Marvys—adopting a more modern, less Old World Jewish name. Such name changes were common for American Jews of the era. Former St. Paul mayor and U.S. senator Norm Coleman, for example, grew up in a Brooklyn family who changed their name from Goldman around the same time, figuring the switch would make it easier to find work.

The Great Depression of the 1930s, around which the Marvys had danced unscathed initially, began to affect Bill. In 1935, his longtime bosses at Western Barber Supply were feeling the squeeze of economic distress. They told Bill that business was so bad he would be paid every two weeks instead of each Friday—allowing more money to accumulate.

An argument ensued, and Bill quit and went to work for a barber supply wholesaler named Alfred J. Crank, who gave him a sales route in southern Minnesota and northern Iowa. Tired of the road, he bounced from Crank to the Empire Barber Supply Company across the river in Minneapolis.

Empire gave him a truck after two weeks, from which he sold his merchandise. But after a year, money shortages swamped the Empire firm. When Bill checked in one Saturday, he was told the company was closing up and he should stop at the bookkeeper's desk to get his final check, settle accounts and take the bus home.

When he got back to the house on McBoal Street, he'd made up his mind. William Marvy was through working for others. He would go out, find his own truck and open his own business for himself. It was 1936.

He asked his eldest sister if he could borrow her car. Then he struck a deal with a competitor from Minneapolis who agreed to sell him merchandise for 10 percent over his cost. Bill hit the road on Wednesday, rekindling relationships with some old clients. By Friday night, he was back in St. Paul, picking up his paneled truck. A carpenter added some shelves that Saturday, and he was set. He painted his name and logo on the rear windows and headed out across southern Minnesota—retracing the old routes he'd started with Western and Empire, by then defunct barber supply companies.

"We sold hair preparations, shaving lotions, barbers' cutlery—whatever items were needed to conduct business—to barbers throughout Minnesota," he would later recall.

Marvy had an awful sense of direction, but he knew his routes. And barbershops were easy enough to find, dotting Main Streets with their array of barber poles. Some were painted stovepipes, telephone poles, water tanks, hot water heaters or simply stripes on a wall. Others were electric or wind-up gizmos with clock-like mechanisms that would keep things spinning for the twelve hours the shop was open—as long as the barber had cranked the key when he opened that morning. Those barber poles were also heavy, with the cast-iron supports and porcelain bowls weighing more than one hundred pounds. As a dealer, Marvy was responsible for installing these heavy beacons when he could convince barbers to invest in their future.

Marvy would stride into two-chair barbershops in Minnesota towns such as Tracy, where Jack's Barbershop might as well have leaped from a Norman Rockwell drawing.

His mantra became "keeping up with the times." As he spread out his combs, clippers and tonic samples of Tiger Root and Pinaud's Lilac Vegetal, he'd urge barbers to look into the future. Then he'd offer a Dutch Masters cigar and go for the kill.

In a 1980 interview with *Time* magazine, Bill Marvy dusted off his old sales pitch for John Skow, a contributor to the "American Scene" column.

"Now you're an intelligent man," he'd tell the barber. "And you might say dollars don't come easy, and why should I spend mine on one of these new illuminated, revolving, high-visibility barber poles?

"And you'd be absolutely right; everyone knows where your shop is. But sometimes a reminder will make a man buy before he really needs to. For instance, you might be walking down the street without any idea of being thirsty, and suddenly you see a sign that said Blatz Beer…"

The barber, shaken down with logical plain talk and longing for that first after-hours brew, would shrug and nod.

"You may not notice an increase in business the next day, or the day after that, but over the course of a year," he'd assure the barber, his newfangled pole would pay for itself.

"The barber needs his pole," Bill Marvy said in 1973. "It not only spotlights his shop among numerous storefronts, it has a subliminal effect on passersby. A fellow spots the pole and thinks: Gee, maybe I need a haircut."

Bill was nearly thirty when he met Rose Goldberg while double dating with other friends. They switched the matchup their next time out, and Bill proposed to Rose on November 25, 1938—Thanksgiving Day and also both of their birthdays. They were born on the same day in 1909 and were married a couple of months after the engagement on January 29, 1939.

For all those years, Bill Marvy had been working out of his family's house on McBoal Street. But after he got married, he finally moved all his merchandise and records out of his parents' home—renting warehouse space at Fourth Street and Broadway in the St. Paul warehouse district for $40 a month near what is now the farmers' market. When a new landlord jacked up the rent in 1945, he struck a deal for $150 a month, with a sliding rental fee based on his revenues, to move into a storefront at 479 St. Peter Street near St. Paul's landmark, train car–shaped Mickey's Diner.

During these years, his in-laws, Hyman and Jennie Goldberg, lived a few miles west of downtown at 960 Goodrich Avenue near the tony Crocus Hill neighborhood of St. Paul. About a mile from F. Scott Fitzgerald's birthplace in 1896, Crocus Hill was inhabited by doctors and lawyers and even contained a little tennis club.

The Goldbergs owned a "bargain store," one of three Jewish-run shops that sold clothing, shoes, luggage and you name it, in downtown St. Paul. While Bill Marvy was bouncing from town to town, hawking barber supplies, his wife would spend the week with her parents, who kept kosher and seldom ventured out from their network of Jewish friends and neighbors.

He'd leave in his truck every Monday morning, returning home—or, more accurately, to his in-laws' home—by Friday night's traditional Sabbath dinner, where prayers were recited, chicken was served and wine was sipped.

When World War II broke out, Marvy was in his thirties, so he avoided getting drafted. He'd been lucky enough to be too young for the First World War and too old to serve in the next one. Although he'd become a Republican in his later years, he was always an ardent supporter of Franklin Roosevelt.

When the president pushed through the Social Security Act in 1935, "everybody complained that they would never get anything out of it and it was going turn our country into Socialists," he'd said years later. "But the Social Security Act was good for the country, and we were patriotic enough to give our support to President Roosevelt's decision to get into the war."

As the 1940s crawled through war shortages, Marvy was earning $100 a week. He knew a lot of people living on half that.

"We were not able to go to the butcher shop and buy whatever we wanted, even if we had the money to buy it," he told a grandson for a historic biography school project in 1989. "We had rationing of food. We had food stamps that would allow us to buy certain amounts of meats."

Those stamps were based on how many kids were living in the house. He had one during the war and two more sons after the battles ended.

"When you bought your meat, you had to pay in cash and give the butcher the rationing stamps. They also rationed fuel to warm your house with. You couldn't keep your house at whatever temperature you wanted. The same way for gasoline."

He was granted extra gasoline because his job selling barber supplies across the state required lots of fuel. The government still limited how much gas he was allotted.

But "there was a certain amount of improper usage of the stamps. There were places that would sell you stamps or sell you gasoline without getting stamps because they had picked up extra stamps from others."

He learned how to work the system and avoid feeling the squeeze.

"The people that had money in their pocket didn't suffer much. The people that didn't have any money in their pocket are the people that did suffer. But a lot of people made big money during World War II," he told his grandson's cassette tape recorder more than fifty years later.

Bill Marvy had bought and sold some real estate to add to his financial well-being during the Second World War. But his effusive enthusiasm began to wane. The road was wearing on him. The death of his eldest son, five-year-old Edward, in 1946 likely prompted Bill's decision to get off the road and start tinkering in his basement.

While most people were content to say, "A barber pole is a barber pole," Marvy was one of those innovative mid-twentieth-century Americans with the creative chutzpah to think he could do better.

He took that first Marvy pole to Chicago in 1950 for the Beauty and Barber Supply Institute's annual trade show at the Palmer House hotel. He and Harris had rigged that first Marvy 55 with a ball-peen hammer, which would bang against the Lucite's plexiglass plastic shell—over and over—displaying their innovation's shatterproof quality.

William Marvy rigged up a hammer to bang the Lucite-framed prototype of the Marvy 55 when he introduced his first barber poles in 1950 at a barber supply convention in Chicago. *Courtesy of the Marvy family.*

From his eight- by eight-foot booth, with the hammer banging until patrons and competitors alike begged him to turn it off, Marvy was at his huckster best—detailing the six ways his new barber pole was better than old ones rusting and rotting on street corners across the country.

In the *Barbers Journal,* he took out advertisements asking questions: "Does your barber pole stand out like a sore thumb in the neighborhood? Ever look your pole over from a distance? Does it look good? Chances are you've overlooked what the years, the weather and the elements have done to your pole."

He appealed to barbers' self-esteem and their pocket books.

William Marvy wasn't shy about drawing attention to himself, as this polka dot suit from the 1970s shows while he sells his wares at a barber supply show. *Courtesy of the Marvy family.*

"Pride in having an attractive barber pole isn't the only reason for replacing your outmoded pole. Actually you'll more than pay for it with the added business from new and strange customers attracted to your shop by a modern revolving barber pole."

His own ego, as substantial as his increasingly portly girth, filtered into the pamphlets and catalogues.

"Marvy will now set the pace and watch others follow."

Prices ranged from $69.50 to $74.50 for the shatterproof Lucite model "that even a rock won't break"—a pitch he amplified for barbers working in rough neighborhoods where vandalism left shop owners hesitant to invest.

Dealers kept 40 percent of the money, or $38.70, and Bill Marvy offered $5.00 for a trade-in to spur frugal barbers to modernize. It was a big price, but Bill backed it up with his trademark bravado.

The Marvy 55, he assured barbers, was "Six Ways Better." The framework was made with non-ferrous metals guaranteed not to rust. For the first time, heavy-gauge stainless steel domes and bowls offered a modern stylishness.

He threw in a three-year warranty, plus a three-way switch and lag bolt for no extra cost. And "the oil-free motor never needs a drop of grease. We defy anyone to burn out a Marvy motor even if it's turned on and run continuously for years without stopping."

He even purported running a two-year test, spinning a Marvy Model 55 around the clock to prove its durability.

Marvy's sales pitch was a strike. Barbers lined up to order poles at the Chicago hotel. By 1952, the *Wall Street Journal* was among the converts. Its reporter at the Chicago show, Robert McCabe, even used Marvy's words in his lead paragraph: "Interested in a 'truly modern' barber pole—'the first real improvement in barber poles in 25 years?' That 'truly modern' barber pole is made by William Marvy Co., in St. Paul. Furnished with a shatterproof lucite cylinder, 31 inches long, it's backed by a reflecting sheet of chrome which produces two more barber pole images. Peering at it, you may get a little tipsy."

Marvy was likely tipsy himself. Within years, he would be running two shifts, making up to five thousand poles a year around the clock. He'd appear on the television show *What's My Line?*, and the *Ripley's Believe It or Not* comic strip on April 22, 1983, would feature a sketch of Bill Marvy holding a barber pole and telling readers that he was the last U.S. manufacturer "of those colorful barber poles."

"Let me tell you, there is value in this symbol," he would say a few years later. "Even an illiterate man can recognize a barber pole. It stands out

Left: William Marvy, salesman and entrepreneur, in 1952. *Courtesy of the Marvy family.*

Below: In 1982, William Marvy, a master of promotion, cracked the *Ripley's* claim to fame. *Courtesy of the Marvy family.*

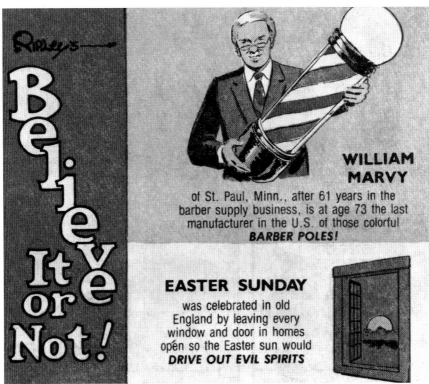

among all the Coca-Cola and Grain Belt beer signs and nobody has to figure out what it means. This is automatic."

He knew a jeweler who once spent $2,000 on a neon sign with flashing lights to advertise his business while Bill's barber poles could deliver its message at a fraction of the cost.

William Marvy smoked his pipe and showed off his manufacturing process in 1977. *Courtesy of the Marvy family.*

"It's a universal symbol with no words," Bill Marvy said. "A child knows it. Nothing tells the story of the barber like the spinning stripe. Everybody knows what it stands for. If you found one in the middle of the desert or on top of a mountain, you'd know there was a barber around."

Not long after he gave that quote to a reporter in 1984 with a swirl of his pipe, Marvy's barber poles would spin in the White House and the Smithsonian. Even renowned CBS journalist Charles Kuralt visited his factory in 1974 for his *On the Road* series.

First Kuralt stopped in La Crosse, Wisconsin—a scant forty-five miles west of Jim Stroh's double pole shop in Tomah. Kuralt visited a barber with an old pole out front.

"Here's a man who can use a new barber pole. But he's had this pole since 1935, and he doesn't see any reason to get a new one," Kuralt told the nation. "With that kind of a tonsorial intransigence in mind, we sought out the country's last barber pole factory to see how things are doing."

Kuralt found William Marvy, then in his sixties, "in a room behind the ancient cash register, seated at his ancient roll-top desk.

"Many trades and professions had symbols years ago," Marvy told Kuralt. "The apothecary had the mortar and pestle, the pawn broker had his three balls, the shoemaker had a symbol, the blacksmith had a symbol, the butcher had a symbol. The cigar store Indian was a symbol for the tobacco shop. All these have fallen by the wayside."

But the barber pole endured, Marvy told Kuralt, and any barber "if he uses his brains, will have a pole in front of his establishment and take advantage of that unique situation."

Then Kuralt, in his baritone voice, asked a simple question: "How long does one of your barber poles last?" Marvy replied: "That's the trouble—that's the trouble—they last forever."

Kuralt ended his report with four words: "See what I mean…"

Although barber poles compose only a fraction of the Marvy Company's business, they come first in promotional banners like this one hanging in the plant in St. Paul. *Photo by John Doman.*

With Marvy making poles so durable they didn't need replacing for a generation or more, he decided to jack up the rhetoric and printed more catalogues: "As modern as a jet plane. Draws customers like honey draws bees."

The Marvy Model 99 claimed to have "more pulling power than the Pied Piper." The Model 55 could "stop the eye and start the sale." And the compact Model 405? Well, "again Marvy comes up with the most dazzling, most attractive, most attention-compelling barber pole ever seen! Modern as an earth satellite, ruggedly built as a bank vault."

2

A BLOODSTAINED HISTORY

His pole with pewter basin hung
Black rotten teeth in order strung,
Rank cups that in the window stood
Lined with red rags to look like blood
Did well his threefold trade explain
Who shaved, drew teeth and breathed a vein.
—1727 book of fables

B ill Marvy never filed for a patent. After all, he might have modernized an iconic symbol. But the barber pole itself swirls back centuries, and barbering has been traced back to the late Stone Age Neolithic period perhaps twenty thousand years ago. Archaeologists have excavated cave dwellings with shaving implements made of polished stone and horn.

Barbering was common enough in biblical days to make a few appearances in the holy books. To wit, from Genesis 41:14: "When Joseph was summoned to meet the Pharaoh, a barber was sent for to shave him, so that the Pharaoh would not be offended by a dirty face."

And later, in Ezekiel 5:1: "And you, son of man, take a sharp knife, take a barber's razor, and cause it to pass upon your head and upon your beard: then take balances to weigh and divide the hair."

Egyptian pyramids from 4000 BC included not only tools but also hieroglyphics on the tomb walls showing how they were used. At Grecian clubs in 1000 BC, friends would meet in lavish barber salons to have their nails cleaned and hair trimmed.

Early Romans introduced the razor around 296 BC to improve sanitation from whatever was festering amid unhygienic beards. All free men of Rome were clean shaven while slaves wore beards—or *barba* in Latin, the root of the word *barber*.

When Caesar arrived in Britain in 54 BC, he discovered men whose only facial hair was on their upper lips. And when barbarians—warring bearded tribes, hence the name, from the north and west of Europe—invaded Rome in the third century, they carried back the Greco-Roman traditions of barbering. That included the surgical duties of wound dressing, bone setting, bloodletting and teeth pulling.

Monks often cared for the sick and used bloodletting to combat an array of illnesses, from sore throats to the plague. But in 1163, Pope Alexander III barred clergy members from performing bloodletting. Barbers, who had long assisted the monks, picked up the slack with their skills at handling sharp tools.

The first formal barbers' association traces back to France in 1252, but barbers were a united fraternity as far back as 1100. They weren't members of a high-status guild, though. Makers of shoes and candlesticks outranked them. Their early unions tried to bolster their lowly social standing.

"The barber-surgeons were forbidden to take part in any official municipal sessions and were classified with such scoundrels as musicians, executioners, grave-diggers, dog-catchers, singers and actors. All were social pariahs," according to Ronald Barlow, author of *The Vanishing American Barbershop* (published in 1996 and dedicated to, you guessed it, William Marvy).

The clergy, who had trained the barber-surgeons in the practice of bleeding, soon turned on them as purveyors of gossip and other sins. Rulers in both England and Germany made public appeals between 1500 and 1621, trying to boost barbering surgeons' standing, but Barlow maintains, "They could not erase the public's contempt for those who sheared and bled them."

Early English charters from 1461 empowered the bishop of London to supervise barber-surgeons as they "labour in the healing of wounds, blows and other infirmities, and in the letting of blood and the pulling of teeth."

During Henry VIII's reign in the first half of the 1500s, barber-surgeons were granted the cadavers of executed criminals for dissection in the Guild Hall. Ambroise Paré, considered the father of modern surgery, cut his teeth as a barber-surgeon in the mid-1500s.

And battlefield barber-surgeons, in addition to keeping warriors shaven, learned practical skills about wound dressing and limb amputation—leaving them more experienced than their civilian counterparts.

King Henry VIII approved a charter for barber-surgeons in 1541, a moment captured in a painting from the period showing barbers bowing before His Majesty.

Ordinances prohibited Sunday barbering, and the laws were strict, like this one from 1605: "No decrepit, diseased or deformed apprentice shall be retained by a barber; No barber is to use more than one shop; No person is to show his porringers, saucers, or basins with blood therein."

As time wore on, tension between surgeons and barbers heightened. Surgeons, naturally, felt superior in skill and social standing. They considered

This 1932 etching and engraving by Reginald Marsh, titled *Tatoo-Shave-Haircut*, shows barbering in the Bowery, or Skid Row, with unemployed men down on their luck. For centuries, barbers have struggled to escape what one expert calls "the public's contempt for those who sheared and bled them." *Reprinted with permission of Whitney Museum of American Art.*

themselves above the lowly tasks of teeth pulling and bloodletting. So by 1744, they had petitioned Parliament, seeking to sever themselves from the barbers. King George II signed an act the next year, divorcing the barbers and the surgeons, the latter falling under the control of a council of examiners from the Royal College of Surgery. Barbers slipped a notch to the status of wigmakers. France's King Louis XIV followed suit, and by the end of the 1700s, European barbers were being eased out of the surgery business.

But the commingling of haircuts and medical procedures lived on in small villages and even crossed the ocean. As late as 1913, a St. Louis barber was still offering leeching services.

The modern barber pole sprung up from this ancient history. Figuring out the accurate history of the barber pole is nearly impossible. Talk to three barbers, and you'll get three different stories about the barber pole's lineage. Historians disagree on some of the specifics but agree on this much: the spiral ribbons painted around early poles represent dual, long linen bandages. One was twisted around the arms of patients to make their veins pop out so barbers could draw blood believed to contain the roots of whatever illness afflicted them. Drawing or letting out the bad blood, they believed, would cure them. The second bandage bound the wounds afterward. Most agree that the bloodied white linen bandages hanging and swirling in the wind near early barbershops served as the precursor to the barber pole.

Others, though, point out that the scared-out-of-their-wits patients would typically clench a staff during the entire operation. That staff would be wound with bandages so it would be ready when needed and hung in shop windows as a sign of what was offered.

Eventually, those wrapped staffs evolved into painted wooden signs akin to the wooden cutouts used by vendors such as goats (for milk), grapes (for wine) and twisted loaves (for bakers).

Earlier Europeans fashioned barber poles with iron spears and brass bowls hanging from them to capture blood or keep leeches on hand for bloodletting. German surgeons wrapped their bloodstained poles with white fur to attract customers.

Whether you buy the bloody rags hanging in the window theory or the staff-for-clenching origin story, the blue spirals popular today are still a mystery.

Some say those trace back to the fissure behind the surgeons and barbers, when authorities allowed surgeons to use red-and-white staffs and barbers blue-and-white bands. That could easily have crossed the Atlantic Ocean of the 1600s and 1700s to the New World. When the colonists adopted a red, white and blue flag for their independence banner, the patriotic fervor ensured a place for the blue stripe. Others say the blue stripe represents the blue blood low in oxygen and carried in veins. The problem is that it is a common misconception that oxygen-rich blood is red and veins are blue. All blood is, in fact, red, but skin diffuses the light and makes veins look blue.

That said, the patriotism theory, coupled with some antiquated English rules and misunderstanding about blue blood, all braid together and swirl around today's barber pole—adding some blue contrast.

Early American barber poles mimicked the British slender staffs with golden acorn-like finials added for pizzazz purposes. They were typically freestanding sidewalk pillars ranging from six to twelve feet tall, according to *The Vanishing American Barbershop*.

But in the late 1800s, barber poles and their cigar shop Indian cousins were deemed public nuisances because they clogged already teeming sidewalks jammed with vendors, carriages and horses. Some local ordinances let these so-called pedestal or pillar poles remain but prohibited any new poles from gobbling up any more sidewalk space.

This 1937 pastel drawing by Peggy Bacon shows a sidewalk pedestal barber pole in Greenwich Village. *Reprinted with permission of Whitney Museum of American Art.*

Tobacco store Indians, like this one in Durango, Colorado, have all but vanished as their barber pole counterparts live on—thanks to the William Marvy Company. *Photo by Curt Brown.*

The Indians moved into the cigar shops' doorways before most were eventually tossed in landfills and rivers, burned in bonfires or otherwise junked. Of the estimated 100,000 wooden cigar shop Indians once popular, only about 3,000 of the sidewalk fixtures have survived in museums and antique collections.

This Edward Hopper masterpiece, *Early Sunday Morning*, was painted in 1930, two decades before William Marvy devised his updated barber pole that replaced pillar poles like the one in the painting. Experts say the barber pole is the focal point of the painting and, perhaps, a stand-in for the artist himself. *Reprinted with permission of Whitney Museum of American Art.*

The barber pole fared better, twirling into the twenty-first century and carving out a nostalgic niche in the country's psyche by fulfilling its purpose: attracting customers with a clean, easy-to-recognize sign.

"Barbershop poles evoke many memories of American Main Street," said David Shayt, the longtime Smithsonian curator of cultural history.

Not surprisingly, then, American art has embraced this icon as well. One of the pre-Marvy, wooden pillar–style poles is the focal point of Edward Hopper's masterpiece *Early Sunday Morning*.

Originally titled *Seventh Avenue Shops*, Hopper painted his streetscape in 1930, showing a two-story stretch of retail shops with apartments above. Cast in dawn light, the barber pole standing on the sidewalk "is the focus of the composition," according to Carter Foster, the curator of drawings at New York's Whitney Museum, which controls the work as Hopper and his wife requested.

For a recent traveling show of Hopper art, Foster delved into historical photographic archival troves to pinpoint the real block in Hopper's painting—which he considers among the top five in the artist's portfolio. Searching hundreds of photos at the New York public library and city's historical society, Foster's eye caught a glimpse of a barber pole in an image of Seventh Avenue between Fifteenth and Sixteenth Streets. It was taken in 1914. Another shot he unearthed from 1926 showed the same barber pole.

It was smaller than the pole in Hopper's painting and colorless in the black-and-white photos, "but it confirmed there was an actual barber pole in front," Foster said, tempering his eureka moment with a curator's calm.

Foster said Hopper lived in the neighborhood and walked by the barber pole regularly before capturing it on a canvas in his studio in 1930.

"The barber pole is anthropomorphic and serves as a stand-in for a human being," Foster said.

With a white ball at its top, the barber pole in the famous Hopper painting looks like a human.

"Hopper was tall and bald, so in a way, it's a stand-in for Hopper," Foster said. "The barber pole holds and captures the strong sun light, casting these long shadows. Infusing reality with a little bit of memory and imitation is kind of the crux of what Hopper did."

Hopper painted his barber pole when Bill Marvy was turning twenty-one, wandering the southern Minnesota roads in his barber supply truck. It would be twenty years before he emerged from the basement with his modern update.

By then, barbershops had continued to grow into more than places to get a trim; they were spaces where men could gather and connect. In his little-known but engaging 1996 book of photographs and words *The American Barbershop*, Mic Hunter writes, "With its familiar sweet smells, soothing snip of scissors and hum of electric razors, relaxed schedule, and idle banter, the masculine environment holds a special significance."

"Think of it as a place of community, kinship, affinity, and affirmation," Hunter goes on. When he asked one barber what time he closed on Saturdays, the barber told him it all depended on the local college football team's success that day. If they were winning, he would close up early and watch the game at home.

"If they are losing, I stay open late because I know guys will be depressed and will want to come in for a trim and a cup of coffee."

Another barber told Hunter the one-word answer to the question what causes traditional barbershops to endure?

"It's not just a haircut," the barber said. "You can get your ears lowered in any of a thousand places. They come for the bullshit. It's hard to come by good honest bullshit anymore, and something like that is worth going out of a guy's way to get."

Barbershops' accessibility, Hunter argues, is their key: "The front wall often consists of plate glass, so you can easily see inside. And barbershops are easy to identify, often by a barber pole clearly visible from the street."

And those barber poles were busy evolving in the twentieth century. Like Americans themselves, barber poles morphed over the decades into fatter, squatter signs. Their old wooden precursors, made on big lathes and painted by hand, fell victim to termites, rot and mass production.

Wind-up revolving cylinder poles begat lighted poles in the early 1900s, and they begat electrically motorized poles starting in the 1930s that can still be spied today.

Bob Marvy has followed in his father's footsteps, selling barber poles and other barber supplies as the owner of the William Marvy Company. His three sons work at the company in St. Paul, Minnesota. *Photo by John Doman.*

But why haven't those poles vanished like cigar store Indians, pharmacists' mortar and pestles, the optometrist's giant eyeglass frames and pawn shops' gold balls? Many people will give you a two-word answer: the Marvys.

"For almost a half century, the William Marvy Company has done its darndest to keep the American symbol alive and well on Main Street, USA," Ronald Barlow wrote in his dedication of *The Vanishing American Barbershop*.

His book is loaded with historic photos and advertisement drawings of barber poles and shops. He dedicates his opus to William Marvy, "who never clipped a lock of hair in his entire life" but made sure "the rotating red, white and blue stripes will remain upon the American landscape forever. Amen!"

Those kind of broad optimistic proclamations prompt mixed feelings from Bob Marvy, William's son who now runs the company. Bob, sixty-six but still a full-time force in the barber supply game, started on the factory floor as a teenager after school and on Saturdays. He traipsed along with his father and elder brother, Jim, to barber supply conventions in New York, San Francisco and Chicago.

He remembers the late 1960s, the Beatles, the Vietnam War and the lean years in the early 1980s, when Marvy barber pole production plummeted from a record high of 5,100 in 1967 to under 400 just fifteen years later. Bob Marvy charted the numbers that show it took seventeen years to produce the first 50,000 Marvy barber poles and thirty-five years to crank out the next 35,000. He remembers how, one by one, the competition died off.

"The Beatles drove a lot of barbers crazy," William Marvy once said. "The old barber was accustomed to just plain haircutting."

3

THE LEAN YEARS

Everybody had a good year
Everybody let their hair down
Everybody pulled their socks up
Everybody put their foot down.
—Lennon & McCartney, "I've Got a Feeling"

There were two barbershops in my town—Glencoe, Illinois, a suburb on Chicago's North Shore of Lake Michigan—when I was growing up. The two shops stood across from each other on Vernon Avenue, the village's main artery. Andy's changed its named to Andy's Hair Styling for Men and still exists. Bud's Barbershop had a sign in the window: "Keep America Beautiful: Get a Haircut." Bud vanished from the scene long ago.

Two weeks into January 1967, far from my Glencoe home and the Marvys' St. Paul headquarters, hippies in San Francisco organized the "First Human Be-In." They descended on Golden Gate Park to "celebrate and prophesy the epoch of liberation, love, peace, compassion and unity of mankind." Governor Ronald Reagan called the longhaired students behind the event "bums," and historian Edward Shorter said they were a symbol of "massive uninterest" in parental values.

Newsweek's correspondent covering the events and the cataclysmic cultural upheaval underway by the Bay, Michael Lydon, received a suggestion from his bosses at the magazine: a haircut might be a condition for further employment.

The nation teetered, and hair length was among its fulcrums. As late as 1972, the California Unemployment Insurance Appeal Board ruled that jobless men with long hair were voluntarily restricting their employment options and thus were not eligible for unemployment compensation.

It was an idea that goes way back to biblical times when Saint Paul wrote, in 1 Corinthians 11:14–15, "Doth not nature itself teach you, that if a man have long hair it is a shame unto him?"

Back in St. Paul, William Marvy had seen the mop tops from Liverpool, the Beatles, sweep to popularity among his kids' generation. And the divide

Called by one barber who knew him "the quintessential salesman," William Marvy's booth at national barber supply shows, like this one in the 1950s, was always chock-full of his signature barber poles. *Courtesy of the Marvy family.*

over the Vietnam War hit him personally. His brother's kids joined the stream of young people running to Canada to avoid fighting in what they thought was an immoral war.

But the red logbooks in the William Marvy Company offices told a different slice of history. With two shifts going day and night, employing more than a dozen workers on each rotation, the company was sending barber poles across the country. Dealers were lining up at Marvy's booth at trade shows. And by the year's end, far from the hippies' "Be-In," the William Marvy Company shattered its annual sales record—pumping out 5,100 barber poles, or more than seventeen each business day.

At a lavish party at the factory to celebrate the 50,000th pole, Bill Marvy sliced a towering cake, baked and frosted to look like a barber pole. He wore a red, white and blue–banded crown and posed for photographs with

William Marvy checked out a special gold pole, No. 50,000, made in 1967. *Courtesy of the Marvy family.*

William Marvy cut a barber pole cake to celebrate the 50,000th pole in 1967. *Courtesy of the Marvy family.*

his first customer from 1950. At fifty-seven, Bill had sandy hair that had started to thin, exposing more and more of his temples. His mustache was showing hints of gray. His belly had grown ample in the years since his hot dog–eating wagers. His bellowing laugh boomed louder than ever while his reading glasses became almost permanently glued to the end of his nose.

William Marvy threw his arm around a client whose name has been lost to history. It might have been dealer George Kimble or barber Stanley Olson, who sold and bought, respectively, the first Marvy pole in 1965; or the lucky barber who ordered the gold-plated No. 50,000, which the company has retained in its offices. *Courtesy of the Marvy family.*

That 50,000th pole was made entirely with gold-plated castings by the workers Bill Marvy liked to call "my men." Toasts were made, photographs were taken and William Marvy took off his red blazer to personally hand out pieces of red, white and blue cake.

Left: This is one of the last photographs of William Marvy, taken in the 1980s. He died in 1993 at age eighty-three. *Courtesy of the Marvy family.*

Below: A storyteller by nature, William Marvy was also known for his barrel laugh. Here, he sat at his old roll-top desk, which still graces the lobby of his family business in St. Paul, Minnesota. *Courtesy of the Marvy family.*

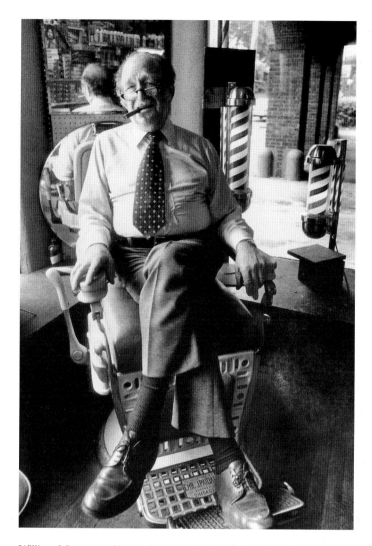

William Marvy, smoking a cigar on a barber chair, reflected on the business's ups and downs in the 1980s. *Courtesy of the Marvy family.*

But the festive mood at the party foretold a massive downturn for the barber pole business. There were roughly 92,000 U.S. barbershops when Marvy and Harris came up with their Model 55 in 1949. The number swelled to 112,000 barbershops in Marvy's peak year of sales, 1967. Within five years, 20 percent would go out of business as the number of barbershops tumbled by two-thirds, to fewer than 40,000 by 1984. That number of traditional barbershops has since dropped below 30,000. There are now nearly twice

William Marvy posed with his poles in the 1980s. *Courtesy of the Marvy family.*

as many Marvy barber poles out there on storefronts and in collectors' dens than there are traditional barbershops.

Marvy's barber poles sales followed the same slide as the barbershops, dropping from 5,100 in 1967 to fewer than 400 in the early 1980s. It took five years to produce the first 10,000 poles and more than three times that long to manufacture the last 10,000.

Bill Marvy pointed to the Beatles and shrugged.

"They came along and long hair was the fashion," he said in 1980. "Before them, you'd have these Jim Dandys going into the barbershop for a trim every week. After the Beatles, they'd go in every two weeks. And a guy who used to go every two weeks, might go every three weeks. Even the older people changed."

The barbers, like crew cut–topped Bud in Glencoe, could be a hard-nosed breed resistant to change. Bob Dylan could have included barbers in with the politicians in his lyrics: "Come senators, congressmen, please heed the call. Don't stand in the doorway, don't block up the hall. For he that gets hurt will be he who has stalled. There's a battle outside, and it is ragin'. It'll soon shake your windows and rattle your walls, for the times they are a-changin'."

And the stubborn barbers who refused to adapt withered.

"What that meant was that a lot of barbers got out of the business," Bill Marvy said in 1980. "And what do you do with a couple of barber chairs and a barber pole? You sell them back to the supplier. So when somebody else needed a pole, there was always a used one around."

One by one, Marvy's competitors died off. The Koken Barber Supply Company had long been an industry kingpin in St. Louis. Ernest Koken, a German immigrant, worked for a factory selling custom china shaving mugs. He was, at his core, an engineer. In the 1880s, he patented a reclining chair and a hydraulic chair, revolutionizing the barber chair. After Ernest's death in 1907, his son Walter helped establish Koken as a full-market barber supplier of all things barbers need: scissors, mirror cases, razors, lather, brushes and barber poles. But the Koken Company went bankrupt in the 1950s just as Marvy's company was taking off.

Koken's office building in downtown St. Louis still stands, although it's now known as the Koken Art Factory. It's teeming with artists and galleries and enjoys a spot on the National Register of Historic Places.

The Koken Company's downfall was linked, in part, to foreign competition. In the 1950s, an Osaka, Japan–based firm named Takara first gobbled up Belmont, another pioneering barber pole firm. Then Takara Belmont acquired the Koken brand and patents in the 1960s. Koken was the second-largest barber supply company before the Japanese takeover.

That Asian competition proved deadly for the other big name in barber supplies in the 1900s: Emil J. Paidar, whose office at 1120 North Wells Street in Chicago's Loop was at one time the epicenter of U.S. barber supplies—including chairs and poles. Paidar barely survived the Depression, staying in business by producing cartridge cases and other World War II war supplies.

But when Takara Belmont, cashing in on lower wages in Asia, started producing Paidar-style barber chairs for 30 percent less money, Paidar's slice of the barber supply pie shrunk. The company merged some of its operation with the Koch company—the legacy of another early 1880s Chicago barber chair pioneer named Theodore Koch. The combined company went belly up in the early 1970s. Other lesser-known barber pole makers in Detroit, Los Angeles and Winston-Salem, North Carolina, also called it quits. In those final years, the Marvy Company agreed to produce its competitors' barber poles under their labels.

A Japanese firm in the early 1970s jumped in the market with a well-made pole that was competitively priced. But Bill Marvy said with some relish that an electrical snag prompted the firm to scrap the idea. Japanese and Chinese makers have emerged in recent years, churning out cheaper poles. But the William Marvy Company's six hundred poles commissioned for 2014 reflect a slight uptick despite the ominous storm clouds descending from foreign competition.

William Marvy's narrative is easy to dismiss as an aw-shucks tale of an engaging, storytelling salesman who happened to come up with a unique innovation: an updated barber pole. But his story is clearly more than cute when you consider how he prospered while other long-standing industry names such as Koken and Paidar withered amid economic forces ranging from changing hairstyles to overseas undercutting.

Marvy was not one to gloat, though. He never bragged about putting his rivals out of business.

"I just diluted their business to a point where they lost their enthusiasm," he said in a 1984 interview with writer Gretchen Legler. "We got all excited about the barber pole business and they were just coasting along. They figured: 'Marvy is making such a big fuss about barber poles. Let 'em have it.'"

As Bill Marvy's quirky niche grew, so did his base of business. After outgrowing his parents' basement when he launched his own company in

In the early days, the Marvy Company had three storefronts in downtown St. Paul on St. Peter Street. This photo from the 1940s shows the barber poles Marvy sold before he started making his own in 1950. Hamm's Beer, another St. Paul product, and dancing were both available next door. *Courtesy of the Marvy family.*

This storefront in St. Paul, three doors from the St. Peter Street showroom, harkened back to an era before the William Marvy Company started making its own barber poles. *Courtesy of the Marvy family.*

William Marvy moved his business from downtown St. Paul to St. Clair Avenue in the early 1960s, and his family still manufacturers barber poles and disinfecting solutions at this brick factory today—the last barber pole maker in North America. *Courtesy of the Marvy family.*

1936, Bill Marvy moved to a commercial loft in downtown St. Paul and then to two storefronts on nearby St. Peter Street, with a third nearby location serving as a retail supply store. He soon had three people on the road hawking his goods, two people manning the phones in the office and a shipping clerk.

Since 1961, the business had been housed in a brick building on St. Paul's St. Clair Avenue in a leafy residential neighborhood near Macalester College. In 1992, the company bought an adjacent building to house its offices. The original building is still the factory and proof that William Marvy knew more about business than simply selling barber poles.

After years in the three different storefronts in St. Paul, Marvy eyed the vacant garage on St. Clair. It had been constructed as a parking garage for an adjacent apartment building that couldn't afford it and poured the money set aside back into the apartments. The neglected garage served as a warehouse for the Excelsior Bakery's home-delivery route. It became Willy's Garage. Ford and Chevrolet dealerships stored cars there.

Marvy's real estate agent scoffed when Bill told him to offer half the asking price—$46,250 in 1961. But the bank said, "Yes," and the eighteen thousand square feet on the main floor became the factory, with a small retail shop, while the disinfectant is made in huge second-floor vats above the barber pole line.

"I have a lot of respect for trying to earn an honest dollar," Bill Marvy said in 1980, "trying to make a living in an old-fashioned business. We just work hard and try to turn out the best product we can: plain, old-fashioned barber poles."

Work, as it was for many of his generation, was Bill Marvy's life. Like many of his era, he wanted to leave things better for his kids, and that meant sticking around the office well into his seventies, processing orders and keeping an eye on things.

"I've never had a forty-hour week in my life,' he said. "I'm not really a great sportsman, and I'm not what you would call a drinking man. I think about work all the time, actually."

And those thoughts turned to adapting to the tough times to ensure his company would survive for his son and grandsons to run. Marvy's company sought out contracts with prisons. It struck a deal with the navy to put poles and disinfectant on ships and at bases. It expanded sales globally, reaching out through catalogues and a web of dealers to barbershops in Australia, Liberia, Norway, Mexico, Spain and the Netherlands—in addition to filling orders in all fifty states.

William Marvy in his office in the 1980s. *Courtesy of the Marvy family.*

The Marvy Company began making small "poodle poles" with spinning pink dogs in the cylinder for the growing dog-grooming market. It has made custom green-and-yellow swirling poles for an Atlantic City casino. It made another with green stripes for a pizza parlor, and a Minnesota Twins model hangs in the Lyon's Pub in Minneapolis, a line drive from the team's Target Field home.

And bowing to the advent of the unisex hair salons that were gobbling up the traditional barbershops' wedge of the market, Marvy's factory starting making poles with the swirling blue stripes and the words "Hair Stylist"—a new product that never really caught on.

Marvy diversified in other ways as well, creating Mar-V-Cide disinfectant, which could be poured into specially designed glass comb and scissors containers—Marvy Sanitizing Jars—to keep things spick-and-span at heath clubs and salons. The company sells those grooming supplies to prisons, hospitals, military bases and country clubs.

The company branched out its supply of neck dusters, "Clipper Ease" aerosol disinfectants, shaving mugs, hair brushes and combs, embracing cultural diversity by selling boxes containing twenty-eight different kinds of Afro picks stacked in the warehouse adjoining the factory along with other hair-care products aimed at African Americans.

The Marvy comb line came with names that started with the word "Ace" and blossomed from there: the Ace Racer, the Ace Flexor, the Ace Expert, the Ace All-Purpose, the Ace Finger Wave, the Ace Crewman, the Ace Redman and the Ace Riteway.

Unlike the pole business, competition remains fierce in the disinfectant sector, where Barbicide—a Windex-blue germ and fungus killer—dominates the market.

Maurice King, the Brooklyn creator of Barbicide who invented the tropical blue juice in the 1940s, also sells a liquid that dissolves hair. He's credited with enhancing barbershop sanitation and lifting it up from the days when barbers wiped off their combs on their smocks.

The Smithsonian Institution's National Museum of American History threw a ceremony—complete with a barbershop quartet—to usher Barbicide into its collection in 1977, at which time, King's son, Ben, presented a jar of Barbicide, some scissors and a hefty donation to the national museum.

William Marvy had always boasted about having a barber pole in the Smithsonian. But his son, Bob, received a phone call after he told the *New York Times* in 1997 that he wasn't jealous about the Barbicide induction because the museum already had a Marvy 55 in its collection.

The call came from a Smithsonian insider who'd checked the collection—there was no pole. Apparently the one Bill donated went to a sister museum, the Cooper-Hewitt-Smithsonian Design Museum in upper Manhattan. It had either been lost or sold by a dealer friend of Bill Marvy's after the museum no longer needed the pole.

"We had a pole at the Smithsonian before Barbicide, but apparently it disappeared," Bob Marvy said.

So in 1998, some seven months after Barbicide's jar of blue disinfectant joined the Smithsonian's vaunted collection of Americana, the Marvys kicked in a major contribution and were fêted at a luncheon, complete with the same barbershop quartet. Marvy pole No. 75,000 now resides in the museum's rotating collection, displayed on occasion.

"It's a symbol of American life," Smithsonian curator David Shayt said. "And it is a complement to our existing barbershop collection."

Sadly, William Marvy didn't live long enough to attend his own Smithsonian luncheon. He died five years earlier in 1993 at age eighty-three. He'd been suffering from kidney disease, and his hip had rotted away. He underwent surgery after a fall to repair his fractured hip.

"He came through it and said it was the best he felt in years," his son, Bob Marvy, said from his large office peppered with antique barber supplies, old shaving mugs and a few wooden poles. His father died of a heart attack the night after talking about how good it felt to be pain-free.

When *National Geographic* magazine ran a story on the Twin Cities in the fall of 1980, it included this photo of William Marvy surrounded by his pride and joy. *Courtesy of the National Geographic Society.*

"A blood clot must have gotten him. But it's OK. He died happy. He was just feeling so good."

Rose, Bill's wife of fifty-four years with whom he shared a birthday, passed away thirteen years later at age ninety-six.

"We are barber pole people," William Marvy said in 1980. "That's what we think about when we wake in the morning, and that's what we think about when we go home at night."

Over the years, the sale of barber poles dwindled to about 30 percent of the company's annual revenues—which range from $1.0 to $2.5 million a year. But manufacturing and saving barber poles, despite what the bottom line said, remains at the core of the Marvy mission.

"We're most well-known for our commercial barber poles, but it's shrunk to a fraction of the business," Bob Marvy said. "It's still our pride and joy."

4

A Visit to the Factory Floor

Babies haven't any hair,
Old men's heads are just as bare;
Between the cradle and the grave
Lies a haircut and a shave.
—*Samuel Hoffenstein (1890–1947)*

The thrum, thrum, thrum of the disinfectant machine upstairs blends with the sound of Hmong folk music playing on a small boombox radio plugged into the wall. Posters of old football players are taped to the gray painted interior of the William Marvy Company factory floor inside a spick-and-span brick warehouse. Of the fifteen employees, most work in the adjacent offices and retail shop. A handful of men make the barber poles and stir the vats of disinfectant. Most have been there for years.

Chue Vang holds a fine-tipped paintbrush in his right hand and dips it into an oozing glue-like mixture of floor filler and water. It's the same caulk formula the William Marvy Company has been using for decades. He delicately dabs the paintbrush along the base of a barber pole skeleton, adhering the glass in place.

Outside on this February morning, it's cold and sunny in St. Paul. The light filters into the old used car garage that has served as the Marvy plant and center of operations for more than fifty years.

Chue is forty-five and has worked for the Marvy family for thirteen years. He's one of three Hmong workers among the fifteen William Marvy Company employees. When the company cranked out Barber Pole No.

Chue Vang, forty-three, is a Hmong immigrant from Vietnam War–torn Laos. He has worked for the William Marvy Company for fifteen years making barber poles, among other tasks. *Photo by Curt Brown.*

75,000 in 1998—a pole now in the Smithsonian—Bob Marvy shut the plant down and took everyone to the nearby St. Clair Broiler restaurant and a Minnesota Twins game. The nice gesture came with unexpected hurdles. The company's Hmong immigrants brought their own rice to eat instead of the burgers on buns at the Broiler. And the Twins game baffled them.

Chue's father fought for the CIA in his native Laos during the Vietnam War, and the family joined thousands from Hmong clans making their way to St. Paul. Chue is part of the largest urban concentration of Hmong immigrants in the United States who somehow selected the land of the windchill factor as their new home after the Vietnam War.

Although the Marvy 55s are the traditional mainstay of the company since 1950, the St. Paul, Minnesota firm makes poles in an array of sizes. These hang in the plant, waiting to fill orders in New Jersey in July 2014. *Photo by John Doman.*

Chue goes around and around with his paintbrush, circling the bases. These barber tadpoles, just clear glass cylinders and aluminum bases at this point, will sit and rest for a few days until the glue and caulk dries.

In a windowed office in the back, Scott Gohr bends over what he calls a mandrel. He's got a title as rare as they come: barber pole technician. His mandrel looks like a massive wooden rolling pin you'd use in making bread. He takes red, white and blue–striped sheets of thick plastic-coated paper and rolls them through the mandrel until they become bonded cylinders. He crimps the ends like pie crust and fastens them with a metal clasp. They used to use striped parchment paper, placing it beneath the glass so that it was tucked inside the cylinder. But those old paper inserts tended to fade and age in the raw weather of Minnesota and exposed street corners across the world. So Scott works with something called acetate sheets—multicolored in red, white and blue—bonded with a solvent during its roll through the mandrel machine.

Scott is fifty-six and just celebrated his thirtieth year at the William Marvy Company. His hair is long and grayish white, pulled in a ponytail that drops down to his lower back. His beard is full and white. He nods at the irony. If everyone had hair as long as his, there would be no need for barbers or barbershops or barber poles.

"Bill was a little bit against the long hair, but he never said anything," Scott said. "It was never like 'stay away from me.'"

Scott Gohr, a longtime Marvy employee and barber pole collector, rolls a cylinder on a new pole in July 2014. *Photo by John Doman.*

New cylinders were lined up and ready to be inserted in the latest batch of Marvy barber poles in July 2014. *Photo by John Doman.*

Many Marvy barber poles, like this Model 77, No. 77,375, no longer hang outside barbershops. This one hangs by the men's room door at an Applebee's in Durango, Colorado. *Photo by Curt Brown.*

It was just the opposite, in fact. Scott was laid off from his job at a battery-making plant in the early 1980s and began working construction. He was on the crew adding the second floor to the factory when Marvy hired him.

"He was a great storyteller and when I started in the shop, he sat me down and spent two hours telling me the ins and outs of the whole process, the business of selling things and production. He was a go-getter, always business conscious and just loved what he was doing."

Before long, Scott became a fanatical barber pole collector himself, with a suburban garage crammed full of wooden pillars and pedestal poles, porcelain-bowled poles and even a neon sign from 1929. He's got a floor model in his living room and another pole mounted in his bedroom. When collectors or antique hounds call for a part, he'll not only track it down but also cross-reference their serial numbers with the red logbooks in the vault to tell the owners when their poles were made. He's been known to trade parts—an engine for a porcelain base deal was recently struck—as repairing and renovating old barber poles for the antique market evolve into a larger share of the Marvy business. About one-third of the poles these days go to decorative uses in dens, lounges, restaurant and offices.

Scott often visits the ledger books, stored on the same shelf in the vault. When I was there, he opened the first one, which includes this detailed notation in William Marvy's neat, cursive handwriting:

First pole delivered—assembled by Wm Marvy. Upright standard 55 hand-painted black. Model No. not shown on plate. Made 2-17-50. Sold by Geo. Kimble 2-21-50 to: Stanley Olson, Rt. 1, Grantsburg, Wis, Returned for service 5-24-50—loose on bottom due to improper fit. Returned to barbershop on 5-31-50. This was the original pole—rebuilt. I held it on our premises for several years—then sold it to George Dennmeyer, 205 E. 4th St., St. Paul, MN. for $90.00.

"That's the neat part, I just love the nostalgia," Scott Gohr said, wrapping another acetate swath of red, white and blue into a cylinder on his mandrel.

It's a short walk through the small retail shop from the factory floor to the adjacent office portion of the William Marvy Company. William's old oak roll-top desk sits in the front lobby—as if he just stepped away for a minute to schmooze a dealer over his favorite lunch: a chopped liver sandwich from a nearby deli.

Although William Marvy has been dead for more than twenty years, his image is everywhere at the offices that bear his name. Framed photographs

These logbooks, kept in the Marvy Company vault, include every serial number, model number and day of manufacture of the eighty-five thousand poles made since 1950. *Photo by Curt Brown.*

hang in a conference room crammed with an unofficial museum full of old catalogues, letters, barbering tools and even an old barber chair. And there are, of course, dozens of barber poles sprinkled throughout the plant: from wooden pillars and crank-up keyed ones to the gold-plated No. 50,000, which hangs high on a wall in the back shipping area.

Bill's son, Bob Marvy, has shared his six decades with all those barber poles. He was not quite two when his father and Bill Harris emerged from the basement with the first one in 1950. Family lore said his dad let him flip the switch.

At the barber supply show in San Francisco in 1956, William Marvy's sons, eleven-year-old Jim and eight-year-old Bob, manned the family business booth. *Courtesy of the Marvy family.*

Amid the boxes and scrapbooks in the conference room archives, there's a photograph taken in 1956, when Bob was eight and his big brother, Jim, was eleven. They're manning their old man's booth at the barber supply trade show in San Francisco. The boys sit in their sports coats, surrounded by barber poles and a sign claiming that these are "The World's Best Barber Poles."

A big man like his father, Bob has kept the business afloat through all the lean years. In 2014, the company filled 598 orders for barber poles, which come in seven different models with various wall mounts and stands. They range from the eighteen-inch-tall Model 410 for about $500 to the signature Model 55, which remains twenty-eight inches with

NOTES ON MARVY BARBER POLES: Marvy Barber Poles have been manufactured since 1950 · Models 55, 66, 77 and 88 had cast aluminum mounting brackets until the mid '60s when they were built with aluminum channel mounting brackets · Models 33, 333, 405, 506, 607, 44, 99 and 824 were manufactured only with aluminum channel mounting brackets · For more information call: 651-698-0726 or 800-874-2651. Have model and serial number available, if possible. They can be found on a small metal plate located usually at the bottom of the barber pole mounting bracket.

MARVY Models 410, 405, 333, 55, 77, 88, and 824 are still being produced.

This page and next three: Barber Pole Identification guide. *Courtesy of the Marvy family.*

Barber Poles on this page are no longer manufactured. Illustrated for identification only.

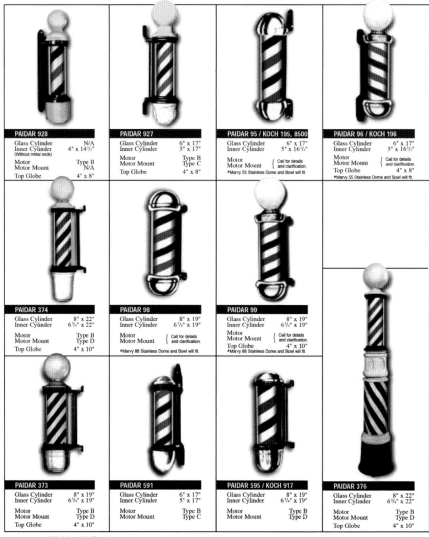

*With Minor Modification

sixteen inches of glass. The two-light model, with a round white globe on top, goes for about $700, depending on which dealer, catalogue or website you use. You can get the granddaddy of them all, the forty-seven-inch, two-light Model 824 for roughly $1,000 through the popular

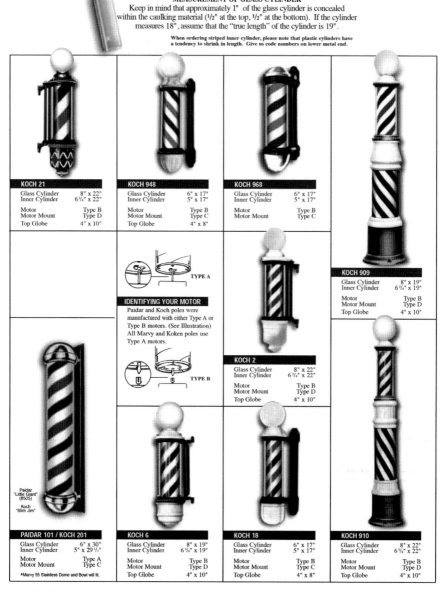

MEASUREMENT OF GLASS CYLINDER
Keep in mind that approximately 1" of the glass cylinder is concealed within the caulking material (1/2" at the top, 1/2" at the bottom). If the cylinder measures 18", assume that the "true length" of the cylinder is 19".

When ordering striped inner cylinder, please note that plastic cylinders have a tendency to shrink in length. Give us code numbers on lower metal end.

KOCH 21

Glass Cylinder	8" x 22"
Inner Cylinder	6¼" x 22"
Motor	Type B
Motor Mount	Type D
Top Globe	4" x 10"

KOCH 948

Glass Cylinder	6" x 17"
Inner Cylinder	5" x 17"
Motor	Type B
Motor Mount	Type C
Top Globe	4" x 8"

KOCH 968

Glass Cylinder	6" x 17"
Inner Cylinder	5" x 17"
Motor	Type B
Motor Mount	Type C

KOCH 909

Glass Cylinder	8" x 19"
Inner Cylinder	6¼" x 19"
Motor	Type B
Motor Mount	Type D
Top Globe	4" x 10"

TYPE A

IDENTIFYING YOUR MOTOR
Paidar and Koch poles were manufactured with either Type A or Type B motors. (See Illustration) All Marvy and Koken poles use Type A motors.

TYPE B

KOCH 2

Glass Cylinder	8" x 22"
Inner Cylinder	6¼" x 22"
Motor	Type B
Motor Mount	Type D
Top Globe	4" x 10"

Paidar "Little Giant" (8505)

Koch "Slim Jim"

PAIDAR 101 / KOCH 201

Glass Cylinder	6" x 30"
Inner Cylinder	5" x 29½"
Motor	Type A
Motor Mount	Type C

*Marvy 55 Stainless Dome and Bowl will fit.

KOCH 6

Glass Cylinder	8" x 19"
Inner Cylinder	6¼" x 19"
Motor	Type B
Motor Mount	Type D
Top Globe	4" x 10"

KOCH 18

Glass Cylinder	6" x 17"
Inner Cylinder	5" x 17"
Motor	Type B
Motor Mount	Type C
Top Globe	4" x 8"

KOCH 910

Glass Cylinder	8" x 22"
Inner Cylinder	6¼" x 22"
Motor	Type B
Motor Mount	Type D
Top Globe	4" x 10"

REMEMBER—the more you tell us, the better position we will be in to send the proper replacement parts.

Bowman Beauty and Supply Catalogue. There are also Models 77, 88 and 33.

"There is no rhyme or reason behind the model numbers," Bob admits. "Just something Dad came up with. None of it made any sense."

Barber Poles on this page are no longer manufactured. Illustrated for identification only.

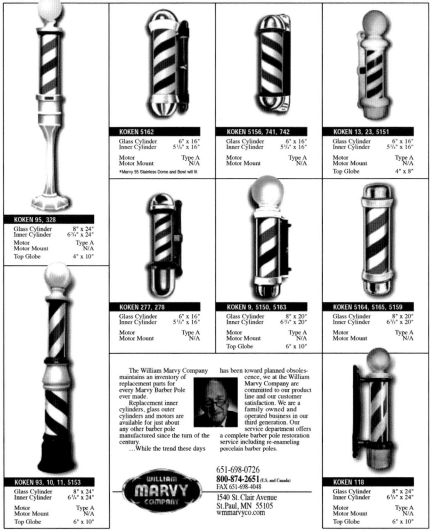

KOKEN 95, 328

Glass Cylinder	8" x 24"
Inner Cylinder	6¾" x 24"
Motor	Type A
Motor Mount	N/A
Top Globe	4" x 10"

KOKEN 5162

Glass Cylinder	6" x 16"
Inner Cylinder	5¼" x 16"
Motor	Type A
Motor Mount	N/A

*Marvy 55 Stainless Dome and Bowl will fit

KOKEN 5156, 741, 742

Glass Cylinder	6" x 16"
Inner Cylinder	5¼" x 16"
Motor	Type A
Motor Mount	N/A

KOKEN 13, 23, 5151

Glass Cylinder	6" x 16"
Inner Cylinder	5¼" x 16"
Motor	Type A
Motor Mount	N/A
Top Globe	4" x 8"

KOKEN 277, 278

Glass Cylinder	6" x 16"
Inner Cylinder	5¼" x 16"
Motor	Type A
Motor Mount	N/A

KOKEN 9, 5150, 5163

Glass Cylinder	8" x 20"
Inner Cylinder	6¾" x 20"
Motor	Type A
Motor Mount	N/A
Top Globe	6" x 10"

KOKEN 5164, 5165, 5159

Glass Cylinder	8" x 20"
Inner Cylinder	6¾" x 20"
Motor	Type A
Motor Mount	N/A

KOKEN 93, 10, 11, 5153

Glass Cylinder	8" x 24"
Inner Cylinder	6¾" x 24"
Motor	Type A
Motor Mount	N/A
Top Globe	6" x 10"

KOKEN 118

Glass Cylinder	8" x 24"
Inner Cylinder	6¾" x 24"
Motor	Type A
Motor Mount	N/A
Top Globe	6" x 10"

The William Marvy Company maintains an inventory of replacement parts for every Marvy Barber Pole ever made. Replacement inner cylinders, glass outer cylinders and motors are available for just about any other barber pole manufactured since the turn of the century.
…While the trend these days has been toward planned obsolescence, we at the William Marvy Company are committed to our product line and our customer satisfaction. We are a family owned and operated business in our third generation. Our service department offers a complete barber pole restoration service including re-enameling porcelain barber poles.

651-698-0726
800-874-2651 (U.S. and Canada)
FAX 651-698-4048

1540 St. Clair Avenue
St. Paul, MN 55105
wmmarvyco.com

The prices range from \$480 to \$1,200 and depend on what kind of mount you get. Older ones can fetch higher prices through the antique world.

"They are a less expensive pole to manufacture than the cast-iron and porcelain poles," Scott Gohr said between cylinder rolls on the mandrel.

"Nowadays, that would be so expensive. These aren't cheap either, but it's a quality pole."

Spoken like a true William Marvy disciple. Scott Gohr and Bob Marvy shrug off competition from China, where cheap plastic poles are being mass-produced and jeopardizing the near monopoly they've enjoyed for decades. They've lost track of other European and Japanese makers who have come and gone over the years. Makers of smaller, decorative poles—aimed for desktops and dens, not barbershop windows—have emerged in recent years. As have makers of barber pole lapel pins and other spinoffs.

The advent of computerized, light-emitting diode (LED) barber poles can't be too far off. It will be curious to see how the Marvy Company, in its third generation, responds to the challenge. Not quick to make changes in a tried-and-true formula, Bob Marvy worries that the company's long and storied use of dealers to peddle its barber poles might fall victim to the Internet.

"We're old school, but our network of dealers is shrinking rapidly," he said. "We used to have them in the warehouse, but now dealers don't stock them. So everything is special ordered."

Years after many businesses went cyber or perished, the Marvys are considering going with a website called barberpolesdirect.com to keep their product vibrant. The logbooks in the vault, containing data that have yet to be imported into a computer system, reflect the old-school nature of the Marvy business.

Making that long-awaited shift to more of an Internet-based business model will likely fall on the shoulders of William Marvy's grandsons and Bob's boys—Scott, Dan and Brad. According to the Family Business Institute, only about 30 percent of family businesses make it to the second generation, and only a paltry 12 percent survive into a third generation. A mere 3 percent of family businesses extend to a fourth generation.

The Marvy third generation, all boys who range in age from thirty-four to forty, have offices and responsibilities at the company. Scott is the chief financial officer and handles day-to-day operations. Dan supervises customer relations, and Brad is working his way up as a shipping clerk. They make the trek to trade shows from Las Vegas to New York just like their dad did with his dad.

"I remember when I got my first badge for the summer show when I was in high school," said Dan, the middle son at thirty-eight. "My dad started introducing me to people in the business."

His father never pushed him, though. Just the opposite: "He said, 'If you want to do something else, you should.'"

The late William Marvy's son Bob (front left) runs the third-generation family business with his sons, Dan (back left), Brad (back right) and Scott (front right). *Photo by John Doman.*

Bob Marvy, photographed in 1997, has carried on his father's legacy along with his sons Scott (middle) and Dan. They are among only 12 percent of family businesses to make it to a third generation. But no kids have been born to a fourth generation, so the end of the line is coming for the last barber pole family. *Courtesy of the* Minneapolis Star Tribune.

So Dan worked for sixteen years at the St. Paul Jewish Community Center, manning the athletic pro shop and staffing the summer activities at Camp Butwin. Eventually, though, the lure of family proved to be too strong.

"It was always my grandfather's wish to keep the business in the family," Dan said. "I realized I might inherit part of this."

He said he never felt the rebellious streak pushing him to get away from the family business, unlike many third-generation business inheritors. Instead, he takes deep pride in telling people he's part of the last barber pole–selling family around.

"People say, 'Oh, you mean those red, white and blue things that hang outside barbershops? You make those?' It can be tough with the economy and getting the respect from the older generation. But my dad went through those issues, and in the end, it's rewarding to try to keep it going."

Chor Xiong, a worker at the William Marvy Company, put his finishing touches on pole No. 84,945 in early 2014 for an order from Toronto. *Photo by Curt Brown.*

As for the fourth generation, well, there is no fourth-generation Marvy yet. None of Bob's sons have children. But customers seem to enjoy supporting a business that has endured three generations.

"They always mention how impressed they are by the longevity of our family business," Bob Marvy said. "And my father would be absolutely thrilled to see how we're carrying it on."

Back on the floor a few days later, the glue and caulk were dry. Chue Vang and Chor Xiong used paintbrushes with shellac and silver paint

Cylinders wait to be added to the newest poles in July 2014 with orders coming in from as far away as France and Kuwait. *Photo by John Doman.*

This serial number tag from a Marvy Model 55 in Rocky Hill, Connecticut, was a gift from a customer to Nazim Salihu, a Kosovar émigré who opened his own shop. It dates back to March 10, 1960, according to the logbooks at the William Marvy Company in St. Paul, Minnesota. *Photo by Nazim Salihu.*

to match the aluminum casings. Scott Gohr placed small rotary motors in the cylinders, and the crew wrapped them up in sheets of bubbled plastic for shipping. All told, the poles have about fifteen major parts—most fabricated away from the factory but assembled in the brick fortress on St. Clair Avenue in St. Paul.

By the end of the week, eighteen Model 405s—the twenty-four-inch, lean member of the line—had been boxed and were ready for shipping to France, where a dealer would distribute the swirling cylinders of glass and stainless steel to barbershops or Americana collectors across the French countryside. The serial numbers etched into the steel plates affixed to the standard's spine were jotted down in the newest of the red ledger books in the vault.

5

A MARVY TRAVELOGUE

You go to any town in America, and the oldest sign you'll find is the cross on the church and the second-oldest sign is the barber pole. After all, it's the second-oldest profession in most towns and the oldest legal one.
—*National Barber Hall of Famer Charlie Kirkpatrick, Arkadelphia, Arkansas*

CHICAGO

In Leon's Barbershop at 8911 South Cottage Grove Avenue, deep on Chicago's South Side, brown and white–checkered linoleum floor tiles match, more or less, the low-slung plastic waiting chairs along the wall—alternating in color between mocha and white. The TV, high up beside a coat rack, airs a National Geographic channel show. And Robert Layne, a career barber from Arkansas who's about a year away from retiring, serves as a mentor for thirty-one-year-old Leroy Young, a former defensive tackle with a tattoo of a pit bull on his hefty left bicep, among other body art.

Marvy Barber Pole No. 20,022 sits inside the front window. A neon sign above it reads OPEN in glowing orange letters.

Back in St. Paul, the red logbook in the vault said the pole, a Marvy Model 66, was completed on April 16, 1960, a few months after John F. Kennedy was sworn in as president. It was sold to Southside Barber Supply, and that dealer, in turn, peddled it on December 14, 1960, to a John Mehan in St. John, Indiana, a scant twenty-eight miles south from where the pole now sits in the window at Leon's.

Robert Layne works at Leon's Barbershop on Chicago's South Side. His Marvy Model 66 dates back to 1960. *Photo by Curt Brown.*

Robert Layne operates the chair closest to the door at Leon's. Leroy mans the second chair—for now. "I'm learning all I can from this man," Leroy said, nodding once with respect toward Robert.

The elder barber wears a colorful necktie underneath a canary yellow smock with green checks. Despite the blinding uniform, Robert is a soft-spoken man. He won't offer his age—"that will cost you ten dollars"—but looks about seventy-five.

He grew up near Woodson, Arkansas (population: 403), where his uncle Wesley Pennington worked as a barber. When Robert was a kid, his father cut his son's hair, leaving silly-looking bangs dangling down his forehead.

"I'd go to school, and they'd make fun of me, call me Rabbit." He chuckled at the memory. He's been cutting hair ever since, starting with his own. He asks the young man in his chair if he wants to "fade it out" on the back of his neck. The customer embraces the suggestion.

Leon Hosley, the shop's namesake, died a couple years ago. "A nice person," Robert said, Leon was seventy-seven and the deacon in his church around the corner. His family still runs another shop nearby and owns Leon's, a neighborhood fixture and community well where generations of men can talk about the world and the block.

In his book *Cutting Along the Color Line*, Vassar College history professor Quincy Mills said the black-owned barbershop provided a critical link between slavery and entrepreneurship.

In the 1800s, most black-owned shops served rich businessmen and political leaders. Both free black and enslaved men manned the clippers. Their shops became "little pockets to sort of figure out how they could at least earn a little bit of money and control their time"—a new reality as slavery ended.

By 1900, black-owned barbershops had begun to serve black men, and they became, Mills said, "this sort of central hub, if you will, for communities across the country to understand the nature of their respective communities."

Robert Layne has worked here for forty years. He's still a member of the barbers' union in a city rich with organized workers. But he misses the days when the once-powerful barbers' association used to control its unique stream of commerce like a lock and dam. Today's union, he acknowledges, is a gasping legacy of what was.

"There are seven shops on four blocks of this street that cut hair these days," he said. "The union used to make sure you were the only one."

The Marvy Model 66, almost identical to a 55, includes its original cast aluminum mounting brackets. It was there in the window when Robert arrived forty years ago. The barber pole, he said, is "an identifying mark. People see it. They recognize it."

An instant message, a nanosecond of neurological clarity, "and the person knows one thing," Robert said, "I can get a haircut here."

His razor fills the silence as his voice trails off. Leroy Young, the younger barber working the other chair to his left, jumps into the conversation effortlessly. It's one of the subtle scenarios that make barbershops so fascinating: the ease with which the chitchat swirls back and forth between customers and barbers.

Sparked by the conversation of Marvy and Minnesota, Leroy recalls his church leading a group of teenagers from his Hyde Park neighborhood to the Boundary Waters Canoe Wilderness in the North Woods. He portaged canoes and carried heavy packs, "and when I got back to high school football, no one could touch me." That prompts laughter from the six of us—two barbers, two clients, a man waiting and me.

In the back of the shop, there's a wooden cabinet display case, a shrine almost, peppered with images, certificates and photographs of Deacon Leon Hosley, along with religious quotes and notations. One, over the mirror near the second barber chair, comes from Matthew 7:7–8: "For everyone who asks receives; the one who seeks finds; and to the one who knocks, the door will be opened."

Chronicling this story about a salesman injecting innovation into the ancient symbol of barbering has opened plenty of doors, including Leon's. Barbershops are open to the public. They foster conversation. In fact, they can easily become an addiction.

My own family members learned to cringe when I'd point out the window and say, "There's a Marvy. Looks like a Model 55."

Bill Marvy could point at a red, white and blue blur out his moving car window and effortlessly determine whether it was a Model 55 or a Model 824. "It's as easy to spot as one of your own children in a crowd," he once said.

My wife would patiently walk the dog in towns like Tomah, Wisconsin, after I'd say, "Just give me a second. Let me stick my head in."

Seconds turned into half hours. First, I'd sit down in the barbershop's waiting area. They all have them: usually a few chairs around a coffee or end table layered with magazines. I'd try to look inconspicuous, which is impossible. Barbers and their clientele can sniff out a stranger. They are used to regular customers. A guy with a notebook is not regular.

But barbers, as a lot, have no interest in stifling conversation. So you bring up barber poles, the walls go down and the stories flow. And I'm not the only one who's become obsessed with tracking Marvy barber poles. In the company's hodgepodge of scrapbooks and mementos, there's a 1977 letter from Joe Francis, a barbering legend and William Marvy contemporary who started off shining shoes at the St. Paul Barber School. He opened a one-chair shop and wound up running the Barbers, a franchising pioneer whose publicly traded empire had swelled to seven hundred salons in forty states and five countries by the time he died in 1994—one year after Bill Marvy.

The letter from Joe Francis to Bill Marvy includes a photograph from Francis's travels to Liberia, showing a Marvy 55 high on a wall along a crowded street in Monrovia. "While I was there, as I do on all my trips I go visit the barbershops," Francis told his pal. "I thought you would like this picture I have enclosed, one of your poles on his shop."

Back on the South Side of Chicago, Robert Layne shrugged off our differences—Minnesotan meets Arkansan—without words, insisting he could cut what's left of my hair. I ease into his chair, hypnotized by the razor's whir, the clipper's snip-snip and the hair spray's sweet scent.

"If we can't do it, it can't be did," Robert said with a smile. "I've cut all kinds."

And I've met all kinds. Here are some sketches of a disparate group linked by two things: sharp scissors in hand and a swirling Marvy barber pole out front.

ARKADELPHIA, ARKANSAS

Charles Kirkpatrick had just returned home from the eighty-eighth annual conference of the National Barber Board Association. He was on his way to the Arkansas Barber Board in Little Rock when he wound up in a car wreck.

"Got bruised up, and they told me I couldn't go to work," he said. Translation: He was sitting at home, bored as a kid in church during a long sermon. He had plenty of time to talk about barbering.

His easy laugh was just getting rolling. Charles went to barber school in 1958 and has been at it ever since. He's seventy-five but doesn't want to advertise his age "because there are a lot of good-looking young women out there and if they knew how old I was…"

He chuckled, slowly and deeply. Charles has two shops, one in Arkadelphia—a city of ten thousand, some seventy miles down Highway 70 from Little Rock—and the other in Hot Springs.

"You know where Hot Springs is?" he asked, teeing things up. "Right under Burning Mattress. You get jokes when you talk to a barber."

And Charles isn't just another barber. He's been the executive secretary of the Arkansas Barber Board for years. He joined the National Barber Hall of Fame in 2003 and remains a bigwig with the National Barber Board Association, a group of gubernatorial-appointed regulators from each state that has been meeting since 1926.

"I haven't been going to the conferences that long, but it sure seems like it," he said.

Inside the front window at his Cutting Edge Barbershop in Arkadelphia, you'll find Marvy pole No. 47,291—a Model 55 dating back to January 18, 1967, when it was sold to the Bopp Barber Supply Company in Little Rock, Arkansas.

"I never met the elder Mr. Marvy, but we all love him in the industry because he's done a great thing for the profession by keeping the barber pole alive and turning."

As he rested from his car accident, Charles offered a slow, meandering history of the barber pole, citing Ezekiel 5:1 for openers: "And thou, son of man, take thee a sharp knife, take thee a barber's razor, and cause it to pass upon thine head and upon thy beard: then take thee balances to weigh, and divide the hair."

He ascribes to the blue-equals-vein theory of the pole's darkest color. "If you look at the back of your hand, the veins look blue. The blood was bad in the old days. So the barber-surgeons wrung out their bloody white towels—the red and the white—and the blue is for the veins. Not to take anything away from our country, but the red, white and blue of our barber poles go back way before that."

He said the wind-up barber poles started disappearing from sidewalks in the 1960s. And the mounted electrical poles outside came inside the shops for a few reasons.

"The long-haired kids wouldn't leave them alone," he said. "They started taking them off the walls to use as fish bowls. When the barber got to work, there was no more pole. They cost quite a bit of money. So it didn't take the barber long to figure out he had to move them inside."

Especially when town leaders began to worry that they were distracting drivers from paying attention to the traffic.

"They came up with these codes and ordinances and threatened to give you a ticket and fine you," he said.

He hung up an eighty-foot flag, advertising "HAIRCUTS" in front of his ABC Barber College in Hot Springs and was ordered to take it down so as to not affect the traffic flow down Brenda Street.

"They got these stupid ideas and passed these ordinances," he said. "But every barber in town has about three city board members coming to his chair on a regular basis. We get the ears of the town leaders. So it doesn't take long for them to do what's right and ease up on the rules."

His laughter returned, slow and easy.

St. Cloud, Minnesota

I waited for my son's friend to pick me up in St. Cloud, Minnesota, for a weekend ride to the family lake place. I'd been interviewing experts trying to reduce childhood trauma for my newspaper job, but it was time to relax.

Barber poles were the last thing on my mind.

I headed over to a downtown St. Cloud coffee shop I'd remembered from previous journeys to this Stearns County seat, a central Minnesota town home to a college, occasionally bizarre crimes and a picturesque name.

I asked a passerby about the coffee shop. He pointed at the building I stood beside and shrugged—it went out of business. I thanked him and sat on the edge of a raised cement planter aimed at beautifying the weathered St. Cloud streetscape. But the flowers were dead.

I took off my backpack, stretched with a yawn and caught a glimpse over my shoulder. A Marvy Model 55 hung high on a wainscoted wall painted dark brown. I would learn in a few minutes it was No. 4966—the oldest Marvy pole I ever encountered in the wild on my modest, unscientific survey. The red logbooks in the vault in St. Paul place the St. Cloud pole's birth on December 14, 1953. That's seven years to the day before the pole at Leon's on Chicago's South Side was sold. And it was the day the Brooklyn Dodgers signed Sandy Koufax.

A dealer named G.A. Singer in Minneapolis made a good pitch of his own, selling this pole in St. Cloud. He must have had a route like the one William Marvy once drove. By 1953, Marvy was off the road, riding the crest of his new, six-way better pole. Part of that boom in business is hanging on the wall by the entrance to a mall on St. Germain Street, a main downtown thoroughfare in St. Cloud. It is one of those 1960s downtown mini-malls turned into a string of antique dealerships.

A hallway circles in front of the small shops, and a staircase drops to the lower level. Around to the right, I met Ray Opatz, the seventy-year-old proprietor of Ray's Barber Shop since 1960. That's the year I was born. And that's a long time to own a barbershop.

He's been located in six different spots, all within a couple blocks of where we stood, inside a windowless nook in a mall across from the courthouse. With no customer in his chair, Ray put down his newspaper and told me how he used to be next to a now-defunct funeral home. Then he moved underneath a gay bar. "Dat's gone now, too."

He let his story unfurl slowly with a thick, clipped accent, echoing his Polish grandfather's. "Tink dat" means "think that." Alex, his grandfather,

Ray Opatz, seventy-five, took over his uncle's barbershop in St. Cloud, Minnesota, in 1960 and was still offering eleven-dollar haircuts and straight-edge shaves in 2014. "The goll dang Beatles raised hell for barbers" in the 1960s, he said. His Marvy 55, No. 4,966, dates back to December 14, 1953, when a Minneapolis dealer named G.A. Singer purchased it with a paper neolite cylinder, according to Marvy records. It's the oldest one I came across "in the wild" while I was checking serial numbers across the country. *Photo by Curt Brown.*

emigrated from Poland in the late 1800s. He jumped off a train in Royalton, Minnesota, and started walking six miles west, across the Mississippi River, toward a village named Bowlus.

"He looked right out of *Tom Sawyer* with a stick and all his stuff tied up in a bandanna," Ray said.

His grandfather met a farmer on his walk and bought a piglet. He vowed to fatten the little pig and give it to the farmer in exchange for his daughter. She was sixteen and would become Ray's grandmother. They had thirteen kids, with Ray's father, George, the second from the end. Most of the Opatz men farmed. George lived on the family's 240 acres just north of Bowlus until he died at ninety-one. Farming, and all the work it demands, wasn't for everyone.

"Three of my father's brothers—Roy, Sam and John—became barbers, and so did their cousin Jim," Ray said.

When he turned twenty-one, Ray said "thanks but no thanks" to farming and bought out his uncle John in 1960. His Marvy Model 55, No. 4966, was part of the deal.

He charges eleven dollars for a haircut and eight dollars for a shave with his straight-edged razor. "Some of these young guys have never had a shave before," Ray said, incredulous. He's cut hair for fifty-four years for one overriding reason.

"No one else would hire me." The left corner of his mouth lifted as he smiled crookedly.

He lamented the unisex hair stylists, the shrinking power of the barbers' union and the longhair trends.

"The goll dang Beatles raised hell for barbers," he said. Ray and his wife, Renee, rent out the old farmstead to a neighboring farmer. They have three kids, six grandchildren and a couple great-grandchildren.

Ray doubts any will go into barbering. Talk turns to the photograph on the wall, showing him hoisting a twenty-seven-inch walleye he caught a couple summers ago.

"Had to throw it back," he said, explaining it was an inch shy of the twenty-eight inches required for keepers. "I tried stepping on its stomach to get it up to twenty-eight inches, but it didn't work."

Ray cracked another wry grin and the phone rang—not a smartphone, but an old-fashioned phone mounted to the wall. It was one of his regulars, scheduling a haircut.

"We'll see you tomorrow afternoon at 2:30 then."

On my way out of the mall, Ray agreed to pose for a photo under Marvy No. 4699.

"Dat's our symbol," he said.

NEW YORK CITY, NEW YORK

About 1,300 miles east of St. Cloud, Jesse Cantillo performs a morning ritual on the sidewalk outside 17 East Twenty-first Street just off Park Avenue. He drags out a seven-foot wooden barber pole and places it in front of Barber Bart. It recently needed repair after a drunken firefighter swung on it and broke it.

"This is our mascot, and we place it out front every morning," said Jesse, whose barbering dates back to a bad cut as a twelve-year-old kid on Staten Island. He begged his mother to take him to a drugstore so he could buy a buzzer and clean up the disaster.

His boss, Bartlomiej Trybala, aka Barber Bart, bought the pole for $800 on eBay about twenty years ago. A Polish émigré from Krakow, Bart wanted to play professional hockey. But he slipped a disc in his back and slipped into barbering. His father back in Poland told him it was good to work with his hands. "He said I should learn to fix cars. I thought about it, but it wasn't for me. Too dirty. I wanted a clean job. I looked at a directory of all the jobs people did and when I saw 'barber,' I said, 'That's for me. Barber. You have contact with people. It's indoors, nice and warm. And it's clean."

His Flatiron shop filters jazz music to customers who sit in $8,000 Japanese chairs with massage and heating elements built in. Appointments are made online and appear on a list on a wall-mounted, flat-screen television. He's come a long way from his days as a teenaged apprentice in Krakow.

"For the first year, you just watch the boss, you sweep up the hair, and you practice, practice, practice," Bart said. "You learn how to give a shampoo, how to massage the head, and you practice shaving balloons. I popped a lot of balloons. When they pop, it's messy. The shaving foam flies everywhere. The good part is the balloons don't bleed."

Since then, he's barbered in London, Chicago and now the heart of Manhattan. He's up to five barbers, and business is so strong that he opened a second shop in the trendy Williamsburg section of Brooklyn.

That's where you'll find a Marvy pole and a twenty-nine-year-old barber named Michael Wood, a third-generation clipper following his father, Paul, and grandfather Anthony.

"The barber pole is our international symbol, and whether it's the wooden one we pull out on Twenty-first Street or the Marvy Model 410 over our staircase here in Brooklyn, they tell the same story anywhere—that barbering happens here and business has been getting better the last three years."

TELLURIDE, GLENWOOD SPRINGS AND DURANGO, COLORADO

Rob Petrie is forty-two. His balding head makes him look older. His wanderlust and zestful past keep him young. A native of Cleveland, Ohio, Petrie headed south, way south, to work as a rafting guide in Bolivia.

He returned to the United States to find the economy ravaged. So three years ago, he decided to get his barber's license at a school in Durango, three hours down the western slope.

He opened the Town Barber in 2011 in Telluride—pronounced "To Hell You Ride" by old-timers—a gorgeous Rocky Mountain mining town that has become a celebrity retreat with multimillion-dollar condos and festivals of film and bluegrass on the Needles Mountains in the San Juan Range.

Petrie's shop is down some steps from West Colorado Avenue, Telluride's main drag. The rent is cheaper when you go subterranean.

"But I wanted my barber pole on Main Street," he said. "And I wanted the best, and that's Marvy."

Never mind that Marvy is also the only. Petrie's pole is a newer model, made within the last few years. It's mounted too high to glean a serial number. Rob's startup is the first new barbershop to open in Telluride since 1973. He bought out a Mail Box Etc. and added nice mahogany shelving. Business is going so well he's thinking about adding a second barber.

When he's not clipping, Rob is collecting old photographs to frame and hang in his shop—a nod to the nostalgia he thinks offers promise for the new wave of barbers cashing in on a male generation seemingly more into grooming than its members' fathers and grandfathers.

One of the sepia-toned photographs dates back to 1906. There's a horse drawing a carriage, some mustachioed cowboys coming to town to spend their wages and a stand-up, old-school wooden barber pole anchoring the dusty sidewalk.

Not all those old wooden poles in Colorado are relegated to old photographs. In Glenwood Springs, 150 miles west of Denver, there's an eight-foot wooden pole perched on the sidewalk near the Doc Holliday Tavern on Grand Avenue. Splotched and faded, the red, white and blue relic with a ball on top easily dates back to the 1800s.

And down in the southwestern Colorado town of Durango, we found four Marvy barber poles in locations that accurately reflect barber poles today. Two hang on Main Avenue, one is mounted at a barber's home and

This old-school, pre-Marvy wooden pedestal pole stands near Doc Holliday's Saloon in Glenwood Springs, Colorado. *Photo by Bill McAuliffe.*

the fourth one—a relatively new Model 77, No. 77,375—resides outside the men's room at an Applebee's restaurant.

No. 62,216, a Model 66, hangs under a striped awning on Main Avenue outside Tucson's Salon de Barber. Inside the window, owner Amador Tucson has been cutting peoples' hair in the same chair for forty-nine years. He was born on the nearby Southern Ute Indian reservation, where his family tree winds back more than two centuries.

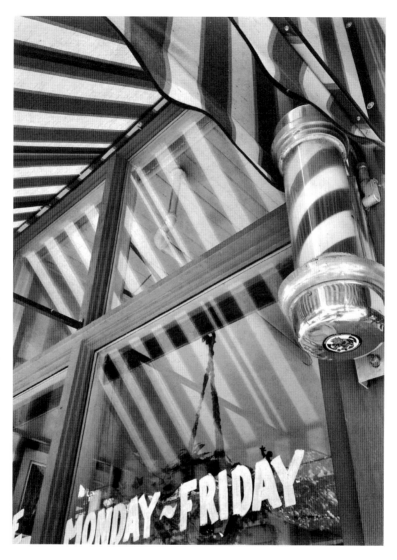

This Marvy Model 66, No. 62,216, dates back to 1977 and hangs in front of Tucson's Barbershop on Main Avenue in Durango, Colorado. It replaced an earlier pole that was vandalized at the shop, which opened in 1903 as the Silver Dollar Barbershop. *Photo by Curt Brown.*

"I started cutting hair on the reservation when I was nine years old," he said. He later worked in Southern California, in a factory churning out trailers, but returned to the Southwest and picked up the clippers again in the early 1960s after a stint at barber school in Denver.

Dating back to 1903, when it opened as the Silver Dollar Barbershop, Amador's two-chair shop has endured the ups and downs of the business.

"I remember coming here in the 1970s when my dad would get his hair cut by Amador," said a woman, waiting for Amador to finish buzzing her son's neck. "That would be his grandfather."

The current pole hanging outside dates back to January 20, 1977, and replaced one that was vandalized.

This Marvy pole hangs in front of a hair salon in the tony Washington Park neighborhood of Denver, Colorado. *Photo by Curt Brown.*

"I still have the old one mounted in my house over in Ignatio," Amador said, promising to check the serial number when "I'm not so busy."

The next day, he reported the one at home is a Model 55, No. 12,244, which traces back to March 22, 1957, when the Five State Barber Supply Company of Salt Lake City made a sale.

Across the street and a few blocks north, a Marvy 99 hangs inside a mall on Durango's Main Avenue. The serial number is scratched off, but it appears to date back to 1971. It's been here since Mervin Bergal took over in 1983.

"It was upstairs by a shop called the Rustic Razor, and the woman who ran it came downstairs and joined us, with her chair and her pole," said Merv, who is seventy-three and lives in nearby Aztec, New Mexico.

The son of Lithuanian Jewish émigrés, Merv grew up in Duluth, Minnesota, but learned his barbering on a navy ship in Hawaii in the early 1960s. "Earned fifty cents an hour as an apprentice barber," he said.

One day in 1964, John Wayne, Kirk Douglas and director Otto Preminger hopped aboard his ship to film *In Harm's Way*. Merv cut several actors' hair, "but not John Wayne's."

After his navy stint, he opened two hair shops in Phoenix before settling in Durango at "Attractions on Main." He picked the name because it comes early in the Yellow Pages and tells people its location.

Amid all the banter and pontificating between barbers and the customers in their chairs, Merv has a story that would prompt a belly laugh from Bill Marvy, who used to hustle home from the road for his Sabbath Friday night dinners at his in-laws' in the 1930s.

More than a decade ago, Merv was trimming the hair of some of his few fellow Jews in Durango. The talks intensified over several appointments and scissor snips, and they wound up forming a synagogue called Har Shalom (Mountain of Peace), which has moved from private homes to rented space in an Episcopal church to a renovated Jehovah's Witness meeting home.

"It all sprang out of conversations that started in this chair," Merv said.

Watertown, Massachusetts

One of the first cities founded in the Massachusetts Bay Colony, Watertown has been around since 1630 and is eight miles east of Boston. Citizens protested a tax levied to build a new stockade in nearby Concord in 1632 in what is considered one of the first tax protests that went down in the

Aneury J. Brito, thirty-three, an emigrant from the Dominican Republic, uses a new Marvy barber pole and a pool table to lure customers to his A Barbershop in Watertown, Massachusetts. *Photo by Curt Brown.*

New World. It would take nearly a century and half before similar protests prompted the Revolutionary War.

At the A Barbershop at Five Main Street in Watertown, thirty-three-year-old Aneury J. Brito is doing something revolutionary himself. He's brought a pool table into the back of his shop.

"If people are waiting, I don't want them taking a call on their cellphone, walking out on the sidewalk and disappearing," he said.

The pool table, he hopes, will keep them around until one of the three chairs opens up. Business has been good, especially on Saturdays. A native of the Dominican Republic, everyone calls Aneury by his last name: Brito. That's the way he prints it on the A Barbershop business cards.

Why the A? Brito shrugged. That was the name of the place when he bought it. And why give up the first spot in the phone book or the websites that lists barbers alphabetically?

Wearing a black smock with "A Barbershop" stitched over his breast pocket, Brito is proud of his Marvy Model 88 he bought for $650 a few years back. As he clipped the hair of a toddler perched on his father's lap, he nodded toward the pole, which is mounted low on the right side of his front door.

"The main thing is advertising," he said. "How are we going to know that's a barbershop? Easy. Buy a pole. The barber pole said it all. And when you're going to invest in something, you want your money to be well spent. Marvy's reputation, year after year, is the best in the business"—not to mention, the only one in the barber pole business.

SOUTH PASADENA, CALIFORNIA

Swarthy's Beard and Hair Design sits two doors down from a gourmet ice cream sandwich shop where you can get taro Nutella ice cream between two homemade white chocolate chip macadamia nut cookies—that is, unless the owner, whose wife makes the cookies in the back, finds your order to be an unsatisfactory pairing, in which case he'll strongly suggest different flavors for you.

Welcome to Southern California. Carlos Jimenez, the thirty-six-year-old entrepreneur behind Swarthy's, likes to "design" hair and quote Socrates: "I cannot teach anybody anything. I can only make them think" and "The only true wisdom is knowing nothing at all."

Carlos had just given a first-time customer a "Pomp," shaping his curly hair into a Pompadour puff up top while shaving the sides over his ears down to a quarter-inch so it resembles a putting green.

"I never thought hair would be how I made my living," he said.

His plan was to go into the exciting field of construction inspection. But even before the housing bubble burst in 2008, Carlos could find "no gig."

His sister, Patricia, "has been into hair since she was a kid" and convinced Carlos to shrug off his inspection dreams and go into barbering. So he went to school and opened his shop.

Everyone calls him "Moreno" because he's darker skinned than his cousins. "But *moreno* has some negative gang-banger connotations, and I wanted no affiliation with that."

So he looked to his Bible. After all, Carlos is currently the choir director at the nearby Light of the World Church.

"In the book of Isaiah, Jesus is described as swarthy," he said.

That's how his shop got its name. During a rare moment when Swarthy's didn't have someone in the chair and someone else waiting, Carlos bounced between topics like a pinball.

He just had Justin Lin, director of the *Fast and Furious* movies, in his chair for a beard trim. He thinks the Beatles weren't the downfall of barbering in the 1960s like so many people claim.

"It was old, hard-nosed barbers who refused to adapt," he said.

But now he sees the industry swooping back as men tend to care more about grooming. He offers an array of extras from facials to hot towels to scalp massages and, soon to come, tailoring alterations.

"There are a handful of places around here where women can walk in and get their hair done," he said. "Men have fewer options. So I went for the male demographic, and that breaks down to about 60 percent Anglo, 35 percent Asian and 5 percent black and Hispanic," he said.

"It's taken like fifty years, but the barbering industry is finally turning around," he said. "I go to trade shows in Las Vegas and Los Angeles, and every year, there are more men's products. Men have simply become more image conscious."

He predicts the next big thing in hair will be the so-called undercut, an Australian-inspired men's hair style with close-cropped and tapered sides underneath disconnected from long, floppy locks up top.

"Brad Pitt was filming a movie called *Fury* in L.A., recently," he said. "So it's only a matter of time."

As for his barber pole, tucked inside the picture window, it appears to be a Marvy Model 405, smaller and thinner than the 55. He bought it from one of his students—he teaches barbering at a vocational school—who said her uncle makes them.

"I'm afraid it might be a knockoff because it was so light with plastic instead of glass," he said. "But it's eye-catching and a conversation starter, and that's why barber poles have been around since the Middle Ages."

"There are four big names in the barber supply business," Carlos said, showing he knows more than Socrates. "Koken, Paidar, Koch and Marvy, with Marvy known for their poles and disinfectant products."

As for his sister, who lured him into barbering, Patricia is now married, taking the last name of Stanley, and she runs a salon in Seattle. And two of Carlos's five children—fourteen-year-old Dina and thirteen-year-old Jared—"just might follow me and get into this business. They definitely have shown an interest. Whenever I try to cut their siblings' hair, they say, 'Let me do it, let me do it.'"

Auburn, California

In the foothills north of Sacramento, more than four hundred miles north of Carlos's Swarthy Barbershop and the gourmet ice cream sandwich joint, Joe Bailon is still working on custom cars—nevermind that he's ninety-one. He's the legendary car rebuilder who coined the "Candy Apple Red" paint color, among other things.

"I'm building a clone of a 1941 Chevy for the next Roadster show," he said.

His car creations have won more than sixty grand prizes at those international car shows. For years, he worked out of a north Hollywood garage and shop on Avocado Street near North Beach. Among his Hollywood customers back in the 1960s were Zsa Zsa Gabor (Rolls-Royce), Dean Martin (Cadillac station wagon), Danny Thomas (Continental) and Sammy Davis Jr. (Vega wagon).

"The late James Gardner would come to my house all the time," Joe said. "He was a sweetheart."

But perhaps Bailon's most famous custom car masterpiece is his so-called Barber Car—which reportedly sold at a 2014 auction for $60,500.

Bailon built the car in 1969 for Hollywood auto wrangler and promoter Jay Ohrberg, designer of more than one hundred movie cars, including those in *Batman* and *Back to the Future*. The Barber Car, an open-topped monstrosity, features an interior of red crushed velvet upholstery, a pair of vintage Koken barber chairs, a working sink and—of course—a pair of compact Marvy Model 410 barber poles flanking both sides of the exterior. He used electrical conduit and rolled it around the chairs, using sheet metal and other materials, including a chrome-plated, four-hundred-horsepower, Corvette V-8 engine seated between an iron rail frame. Joe painted it pearl white and connected a then-state-of-the-art stereo.

"It came out real pretty," Joe said of his creation, which has been housed in museums from the Darryl Starbird National Rod & Custom Hall of

This page and next: The Barber Car was built in 1969 by Joe Bailon for Hollywood auto wrangler and promoter Jay Ohrberg, designer of more than one hundred movie cars, including those in *Batman* and *Back to the Future*. The Barber Car, which recently sold at auction for $60,500, features an interior of red crushed velvet upholstery, a pair of vintage Koken barber chairs, a working sink and a pair of Marvy Model 410 barber poles flanking both sides of the exterior. *Photo by Fred Childers.*

Fame Museum in Afton, Oklahoma, to the Petersen Automotive Museum on Wilshire Boulevard in Los Angeles.

Joe can't remember whose idea it was to order a couple barber poles for his car, but his memory is drill-bit smart at age ninety-one. The youngest of ten kids, Joe was born in Newcastle, California, near his current home in Auburn.

"My father was a railroader, so we lived in a house on top of a Pacific Railroad tunnel," Joe said. "I still go up there and see it." Joe worked in a shipyard before being drafted into the army and shipped to Guadalcanal during World War II.

He'd already been tinkering with cars for years. When he was six years old, he couldn't afford a ten-cent toy car. So he built one out of wood that used cans from canned hams for wheels.

"My first custom car was a Model A I rebuilt in 1937, and I've been at it ever since," he said.

SYLVANIA, OHIO (VIA SUN CITY CENTER, FLORIDA)

John Wooden, the fabled UCLA basketball coach, was famous for advocating the bounce pass—where players could make defenders' heads swivel by bouncing the ball among them. Here is the barber pole tracker's version of a bounce pass. Prepare to bounce around a little in this one, from Ohio to Florida and back to Ohio—the home of the National Barber Hall of Fame.

Peggy Schmidt, a Minnesota barber school maven whom you'll meet in upcoming pages, told me to call Howard Warner, Ohio's barber board director, who in turn gave me the number of Clyde Schafer.

Clyde's father worked in a factory that made compressors for huge air conditioners. Back in high school in Metamora, Ohio, Clyde realized that going to a university wasn't in his future plan: "[I] knew I wasn't college material and I'd have to find something else to do."

This was in the 1950s when barbershops were at such a peak that there was a two-year waiting period to enroll in barber school. So as a high school sophomore, Clyde signed up. When his turn came, barber school officials said he had to start in three days, and he said, "I'll be there."

He soon opened the Clipper Barbershop on Main Street in Sylvania, Ohio—buzzing necks and clipping bangs near Toledo for forty years. His role in the industry soared from there, with nearly nineteen years on the state barber board, a term in the 1990s as the Ohio barber inspector and a 1993 election as chairman of the National Association of Barber Boards of America. All that landed Clyde in the National Barbers Hall of Fame in 2002.

The hall of fame is tucked in the National Barber Museum in Canal Winchester, Ohio, near Columbus—atop the Wigwam Restaurant and an older barbershop that has changed names over the years from Zeke's to the Rex and dates back to the 1870s.

The upstairs museum is loaded with old Koken chairs and a closet-sized hall of fame. The collection—available for viewing through appointments only—includes a Civil War–era folding barber chair, countless implements, an extensive library and more than seventy-five barber poles. They range from wooden to porcelain, and there is even one electrical one with a clock built into the lighted globe on top. Marvy No. 74,999 is in there, too.

"The 75,000th is in the Smithsonian, so we have the one right before it," said Mike Ippoliti, the director of the museum and hall of fame. He's never leveled a sideburn, but as the director of the area's historical preservation panel, Mike took over the museum and hall of fame in 2006, when its founder—longtime barber and Ohio Barber Board director Edwin Jeffers—passed away.

"I've learned more about barbering than I ever wanted to know," said Mike, who is sixty-seven.

Barbering school groups from Charleston, West Virginia, to Manhattan are among the most recent visitors to the museum, he said. Photos of the hall of famers are framed in a rear alcove.

Clyde Schafer joined William Marvy, Hall of Fame class of 1982, in their industry's elite fraternity twenty years after the barber pole magnate.

"The hall of fame is for people who did something extraordinary for the barbering industry," Clyde said. "And they figured saving the barber pole was a pretty good achievement."

Clyde never met William Marvy. "But I've been to their spot in Minnesota. I have met the son and grandsons, and their name was always associated with a classy business [that stands] behind their products," he said. "People nowadays want a barbershop haircut, not some unisex thing, and those Marvy barber poles are a symbol for that."

Ed Jeffers, who started the museum over the Wigwam Restaurant, asked Clyde, a longtime pal, to take over when he retired.

"I did that for five years and said, 'I've got to get out of here.'"

He retired in 2000 and moved forty miles south of Tampa, Florida, to Sun City Center. That's where I found him, at age seventy-three, still cutting hair as a fill-in—so much for retirement.

Clyde mentioned that his old shaving grounds, the Clipper Barbershop, was not only still in business in Sylvania but is also run by his son, Mark, and brother, Ron. They both work there in a shop loaded with barber memorabilia, including three hundred shaving mugs, tonic bottles and an ancient three-and-half-foot-tall wooden barber pole on a four-inch base.

I found Mark, Clyde's fifty-two-year-old son, between trims at the Clipper. We also found Marvy Model 88, No. 8688.

"For us in Ohio, it's not only a symbol, but it's required for traditional barbershops to display a barber pole near the front door," Mark said. "At least that's what I've always been told."

When Clyde retired, his son bought him out. And Clyde's brother works the second chair.

"It's a good family business," Mark said. But he doubts any of his three kids will follow suit to make it a three-generation business.

"As I foresee the industry changing, I think it would be hard for them to make a living," he said. "Society has changed to a fast-food culture. If you ask someone to come back tomorrow because you're busy today, forget it. I've got a loyal five hundred customers I can depend on. But in the future?"

Nevermind the future—let's get back to Marvy Model 88, No. 8688. It was produced on January 3, 1956, about the same time as one of the poles in Tomah, Wisconsin. It was sold to the Windie Barber Supply Company in Dayton, Ohio, 150 miles south of Sylvania. The pole was originally sold to

Roger Dawn of Dayton on March 14, 1956, according to the ledger books back in St. Paul.

So how did it end up in the Clipper? "I got that pole off a building in Toledo," Clyde said. "It didn't work."

He bartered with the barber who owned it. "I told him I'd like to buy it and he said, if I'd buy him a little one for the window, he'd do the deal even up." Clyde recalls finding an inexpensive little window model. "Back in those days, you could get a little one, about a foot high, for forty or fifty bucks at the most."

He put a new Marvy motor in the old pole from Toledo, refurbishing No. 8688, which swirls on outside the Clipper on Sylvania's Main Street.

St. Paul–Minneapolis and Bloomington, Minnesota

About a mile northwest of the William Marvy Company's brick headquarters, just west of the Art Deco Grandview movie theater, a large Marvy 824 hangs from a pole out of the range of vandals, thieves and college fraternity boys who've been known to steal barber poles to illuminate their frat houses.

It's No. 49,373, which dates back to the autumn of 1967. Better yet, the barber inside, seventy-year-old Gilbert (Gib) Peppin, knew William Marvy personally. "Great guy. Smoked cigars and liked to talk about the good-old days," said Gib.

For Gib, the good-old days meant barbering with his dad, Henry Peppin, who was born in 1908 in tiny Dorothy, Minnesota—population twenty-five—tucked up in the northwest corner of the state near Thief River Falls. Henry cut hair until the Depression dried up customers and sent him back to the farm and then down to the Twin Cities.

He opened a shop near University and Snelling Avenues in St. Paul, a half mile from the long-gone Family Barbershop, which opened in 1920 under the ownership of a German immigrant with a third grade education who baled hay one summer to earn money to go to barber school. His name was Carl Fredrich August Schulz, and his son, Charles (aka Sparky), went on to sketch the *Peanuts* comic strip.

Gib joined his father at the University Avenue shop fifty years ago at age twenty-one; they worked side by side until Henry retired in 1988. Gib lost the shop three years ago when forces conspired to make way for a Habitat for Humanity office. Gib's father died in 2013.

But Gib is still at it, now paying the bulk of the rent at the Grandview Barbershop on Grand Avenue. He flashed back some thirty years and remembered Marvy stopping by. Gib showed him a flattop comb from a competitor named John Oster. (Oster emigrated from Sweden at fifteen and settled in Chicago. He soon found work as a tool and dye maker manufacturing blades for hand and electric clippers in Wisconsin in 1921. Three years later, he patented the first portable motor-driven electric clipper with detachable and interchangeable blades. He added the Oster lather machine in 1937. He worked on these innovations when he wasn't developing the top Brown Swiss cattle herds in the country. The clipper and the lather machine, more than the cows, earned him the first spot for a non-barber in the National Barber Hall of Fame in 1972—a decade before Bill Marvy.)

It would be nice, Gib told Bill Marvy, if the Oster flattop comb were pierced with a hole in its handle so barbers could hang it up near their chairs for easy access. Bill Marvy took the comb and put it in his pocket.

"Two months later, Bill stops with two boxes of flattop combs, made from nice molded plastic with a hole for hanging. Of course, it said M-A-R-V-Y right along the part you put in your hand. He had refined it with a hook handle, something nobody else did. No matter what edge he could find, Bill would take it," said Gib.

If you picked up by now that men dominate the barber culture, you'd be right. But nothing is 100 percent.

I stopped by Schmidty's Barbershop, which sits cater-corner from Cretin-Derham Hall High School in St. Paul, Minnesota. A bunch of big-name athletes have come through Cretin, including multiple-year Major League Baseball batting champion Joe Mauer of the Minnesota Twins. He still gets his haircut at Schmidty's.

John Schmidt was friendly enough between cuts. He said he'd tell me what he could, "but you should really talk to my mother."

Across the Mississippi River, Peggy Schmidt runs the Minnesota School of Barbering on University Avenue. Her storytelling prowess rivals only her ability to collect barber poles. She has thirty scattered around the sinks and nooks where not only are barbers trained but also the public is invited for cheap trims from her pupils.

Peggy has a porcelain and stained-glass barber pole that is more than a century old. And of course, she has an array of Marvys, including Model 55, No. 7,004, made in February 1955 for a dealer from the Siskin Company, who, in turn, peddled it to a St. Paul barber named Cecil Sanders.

Her school, started in the 1980s after her divorce, thrust her into a man's world—one she conquered with a no-nonsense, take-charge zeal. Compact as a fireplug, she has a zest for barbering and its poles. She's known in Minnesota barbering circles as the "Barracuda" for her style that's as direct as one of her straight-edged razors.

"People say the American barbershop is dead. But I got news for you: it's not dead," she said. "Like anything else, it's a pendulum."

Collecting barber poles has an ebb and flow, too, Peggy said, pointing to one she found when she was returning from purchasing her father's tombstone with her sister. In an antique barn near Fargo, North Dakota, her sister said, "Oh, look."

"I said, 'Shhh' and walked around and asked the dealer, 'What's that?'" Peggy knew, of course, that it was a gaslight barber pole made with stained glass. She was salivating but playing it cool. She finally asked, "How much?" The dealer said $300.

"I paid him and told my sister: 'Let's get out of here.' They sell for $3,500 easy."

Peggy became the first woman elected to the national barber governing body, which calls itself the National Organization of Barber Board Examiners—sounds invasive. She's testified for bills that restrict barber pole displays to traditional barbershops, a measure adopted in Minnesota and other states.

"If you have some golden arches over your junk shop, McDonald's wouldn't care," she said. "But start selling hamburgers under those arches, and it will take all of a day and a half until lawyers show up to get those arches down."

Unisex hair stylists, she said, are not barbers and are neither trained nor regulated as stringently. "It's a different approach," she said. "Hair stylists deal with frilly, soft and wispy hair. When a barber does a haircut, it's done with a man in mind—balanced and symmetrical. It's manly man as opposed to fluff and buff."

Peggy remembered fondly when Bill Marvy would invite to his factory the twenty would-be barbers enrolled in her class.

"He'd talk about the industry, and you could tell how much he loved it," she recalled. "Dear friend. Great guy. He wasn't even a barber, but he was enshrined in the Barber Hall of Fame in Ohio."

That life achievement award came in 1982, placing Bill Marvy in the vaunted company of some sixty barbers. By comparison, the Professional Football Hall of Fame a couple hours northeast has five times as many inductees.

Bill Marvy was sheepish about his hall pass, jotting off a note to the judges: "I'm highly honored, but I have to tell you a little secret—I'm not really a barber."

They were well aware of his pioneering and surviving legacy and responded thusly: "You, Mr. Marvy have been instrumental in holding for this industry a trade symbol known to no other industry: the barber pole."

Of course, Marvy knew he played his part in saving the barber pole. In fact, he relished his obscure spot in history, saying in 1972: "Folks in my line of work say that if I hadn't improved the old-time barber pole back in 1950 we just might have lost it, too."

Peggy Schmidt, surrounded by more than two dozen barber poles interspersed with her students learning an ancient trade, relishes her memories of a man she calls by his first name.

"I liked Bill because he was the quintessential salesman and knew how to do customer service," Peggy said. "He was a hustler; a fast-talking guy."

And what she remembers most is this: "You never walked away from Bill without something in your hand, a comb usually. Every time you'd see him, he'd give you a comb."

Emblazoned, no doubt, with his adopted name from the 1930s: Marvy.

While riding my bike in northeast Minneapolis—a suddenly hip area where artists and young people have replaced factory and brewery workers—I saw Marvy barber pole No. 32,375, a Model 55.

Back in the Marvy vault, I dated the pole to 1962 and saw

Minneapolis barber Kelly Sharp prays every night that her low-hanging barber pole won't get vandalized. The pole dates back to 1962. *Photo by Curt Brown.*

a familiar name. Dealer Scott Siskin of Minneapolis bought the pole on December 17, 1962, and sold it the day after New Year's Day 1963 to a barber named Palmer.

Mr. Siskin sold another Marvy 55 now mounted in Peggy Schmidt's school a few miles away. That sale was nearly eight years earlier, showing a slice of stability selling hair-care products and Marvy poles in the 1950s and '60s.

At Kelly Sharp's barbershop in northeast Minneapolis, Marvy pole No. 32,375, dates back to December 17, 1962. "You can't have a barbershop without a barber pole," Sharp said. "When it's spinning, it's a work of art." *Photo by Curt Brown.*

I returned to the shop in Nordeast, as the locals call it, and met Kelly Sharp, the female owner of the Barbershop. A former real estate broker, Kelly went to barber school, opened her shop in 2010 and is now a master barber.

She did it, in part, because she wants to preserve a tradition she sees as slowly "fading into a bygone era." Her prices range from twenty-two to fifty-five dollars for "a forty-five-minute, ultimate shave experience"—complete with neck-and-shoulder massage, steamed towels and "essential oils."

I think back to Jim Stroh's Barbershop in Tomah, Wisconsin, with its taxidermy case showing a stuffed fawn; the pool table in the shop near Boston; and Ray, with his walleye photo up in St. Cloud, snipping through his fifty-fourth year. Compared to those old-time, male bastions, Kelly and her shop represent the new wave in barbering—updated, modern and inclusive.

Every night, Kelly says a special prayer. "Hail Marys for my barber pole," she said. She asks God to keep it safe from vandals or stupid neighborhood kids daring one another to mess with No. 32,375. Her pole is mounted only about five feet off the ground.

"You can't have a barbershop without a barber pole," she said. "It's a piece of history, a work of art. When that pole is spinning you know that's a place where you can get a haircut."

Brian Franke has two Marvy Model 55s framing his shop in Bloomington, Minnesota. *Photo by Richard Fohrman.*

Our final stop in the Twin Cities area takes us to the Family Barbershop on Nicollet Avenue in Bloomington, south of Minneapolis and St. Paul and not far from the Mall of America.

That's where Brian Franke, a forty-year-old master barber, holds court in a brick shop with a large plate glass window framed with a pair of Marvy Model 55s topped with the lighted globes of the "two-light" model.

Brian, with tattooed arms and a crew cut, never dreamed he'd be a barber growing up in Scottsbluff, on the western edge of Nebraska near the Wyoming line. He trained as a fiber-optic technician and spent time on a cod-processing boat in the Bering Sea off Alaska.

"My grandpa used to cut my hair, and he sucked at it," Brian said. "So when I was seven years old and started working, mowing lawns and shoveling snow, I went to the barbershop where he got his haircut and spent five bucks on my first haircut."

Before he went to Alaska, he talked hair for an hour with "a beautiful blonde woman" who trimmed him up in Seattle. When he returned to Minnesota, he was reluctant to go to cosmetology school because "I'm not gay, not that I have any problems with that lifestyle, but it's not me."

His barber in Plymouth, Minnesota, assured him there were barber schools where heterosexuals could learn the ancient trade. So he signed up to attend Peggy Schmidt's School of Barbering thirteen years ago.

Now, he's part of that transition across the country, with younger guys and women like Kelly Sharp supplanting the barbers like Robert Layne in Chicago, Ray Opatz in St. Cloud and Charlie Kirkpatrick in Arkadelphia.

"About 60 percent of barbers are over sixty years old, and the highest demographic coming out of the barber schools are younger, black students," Brian said. "It's a transition for the industry."

But his three-chair shop is buzzing on a Saturday with men waiting.

"We're keeping the lights on," he jokes later, after the shop closes. "Hard work has never bothered me. I've worked the fishing boats in Alaska, laid fiber-optic cables and this job—a lot of people couldn't stomach."

Brian said he's cursed with a sensitive nose: "So when old guys come in, they often stink. We've got pimply people, dry skin and stinky customers. Ninety percent of the customers are great, but the other 10 percent can be disgusting. But at the end of the day, they're putting money in your pocket so you stomach through."

Rocky Hill, Connecticut

Nazim (Noli) Salihu said there were no Marvy barber poles in his native Kosovo. But he owns three of them now. The oldest, a Model 55, No. 22,212, was a gift from a customer and dates back to a March 10, 1960 sale to a New York dealer, making it a same-year peer to the one hanging in Leon's front window on the South Side of Chicago.

A gregarious immigrant of forty-eight, Nazim was trained in the art of barbering in Macedonia. When his shop in Kosovo was bombed in 1999, Nazim, a Muslim, fled the conflict and the ethnic cleansing and cut hair at refugee camps in Macedonia, translating for English-speaking journalists who eventually helped him immigrate with his wife and five kids to Minnesota.

There, he met Ken Kirkpatrick, the only other Minnesotan in the Barbershop Hall of Fame in Ohio—besides William Marvy, that is, who was inducted twenty-four years earlier.

Ken runs two high-profile shops in the Twin Cities, one at the airport and another at the state capitol, where his basement shop trims the locks of state leaders and sports a couple ancient wooden barber poles. Ken also has a huge heart and took Nazim under his wing, helping his family find housing and furniture. He paved the path for Nazim to get his barber's license, hired him to work at the airport and, seven years later, helped him earn U.S. citizenship.

That's when Nazim decided to move to Hartford, Connecticut, which has a large Kosovar population and cheaper fares back to Pristina, Kosovo, where he travels frequently. He started working at a small barbershop in Hartford, and things went well enough that he opened a larger, brick corner shop—Noli's Hair Salon on Main Street in Rocky Hill, right off the freeway roughly halfway between Boston and New York City.

"Business has been great with people coming in on their way between the two cities—because, believe me, the traffic never stops around here," he said. "And I am right next to a CVS drugstore, so I have good visibility."

His Marvy 77 hangs high on the corner so CVS customers and people driving by in all directions "can see my sign and know, here's a barbershop." His other pole is perched near the door around the corner. And the old 55 he received as a gift is currently in the basement, waiting to be mounted.

His shop is really two in one, with a modern salon taking up most of the space but an old-fashion barbershop with an 1899 Koken chair and other antiques "for older men who might want to step back in time and have a traditional barber experience."

Nazim insists he's blessed. Business has been good fifteen years after fleeing Kosovo with little more than the clothes he was wearing. He now has enough customers to hire some special sidekicks. His twin twenty-five-year-old daughters, Alma and Leonora, now work at Noli's, as does his-twenty-one-year-old son, Urim.

"I came with nothing and now own a large house in America," he said. "I learned about the Marvys back in Minnesota and learned a little of the family history. They were immigrants, too."

Mair Mairovitz left Latvia, about 1,500 miles due north of Kosovo, in 1903. Nazim made the trip in 1999. Offspring of both men went into the hair business. And roughly in the middle of those immigration tales, Bill Marvy climbed the basement stairs with his barber pole.

Epilogue

It was in special places such as the school room, the factory floor, the front porch, the backyard—and the barber (and beauty shop)—that cultural practices and values were transferred, and transformed, across generations.
—*Norm Rosenberg, history professor, Macalester College, from the foreword of Mic Hunter's* The American Barbershop

One day at the Marvy factory, Scott Gohr leaned over a workbench holding the company's smallest model, the eighteen-inch 410 wall mount. It includes ten inches of glass and sticks out eight inches from the wall.

"This one here is unique," Scott said, his cloud-gray ponytail dangling down his back.

Unique? That means one-of-a-kind. What can be unique for a company that has cranked out eighty-five thousand barber poles by hand the last sixty-four years?

"Usually we keep a hole in the bottom in case moisture gets inside, we leave a way for it to get out," he said. "And usually we put a little motor inside to make it spin."

Not this Model 410. The reason was as a sweet as it was slightly morbid.

Down near Tampa, Florida, in a town called Valrico, fifty-eight-year-old Michael Taylor sells wholesale fuel at a maintenance facility and truck stop. His wife, Michelle, owned the popular Hair We Go salon for twenty years.

"Her whole life story was working with hair," Michael said. "That was her passion."

Michelle died as a result of Huntington's disease, which robbed her of her muscle coordination, in August 2013. She was only fifty-six.

"I had to get my composure, but I wanted to do something special as a tribute and honor to her life," he said. They'd been married twenty-eight years.

Then he got an idea.

"I was thinking of a unique urn to make for her ashes after she was cremated. It took a while, but the only thing I could come up with was a barber pole. That was her life."

He asked his funeral director, who shook his head and said there was no such thing on the market. He talked to some people he found online, but they said "not many barber poles are made any more because people steal them for fraternity party clubhouses."

Then Michael Taylor heard about the William Marvy Company some 1,500 miles north in Minnesota.

"I researched them online and learned that they were one of the oldest companies, and I talked to a few people who said the quality of their poles was like no other."

For $450, he ordered the pole to which Scott Gohr was gently applying glue from his tiny paintbrush.

A few weeks later, Michael was showing the custom-made Marvy 410 to his sisters-in-law and co-workers from his late wife's salon.

"They were all tickled to death and impressed, and it's actually just about the perfect tribute."

He put some mementos and photos in the cylinder along with his wife's ashes and mounted the makeshift urn in her bedroom upstairs.

"I thought about the living room or the mantel, but her dressing room was where she styled her hair. She would just absolutely love it. I took my time, and it was well thought out. And I couldn't think of a better way to honor her."

So Scott Gohr, the ponytailed barber pole technician on the Marvy factory floor, was right. Marvy Model 410, No. 84,942, is unique all right.

What Others Have Said About Marvy

Never one to shy away from free publicity, William Marvy sat for countless interviews after emerging from this basement shop with the first Marvy 55.

Here are some excerpts from stories that sprang from those interviews he granted over the years:

"In a room behind the ancient cash register, seated at his ancient rolltop desk, advised by his son Bob—who will inherit the business if there is anything left to inherit—William Marvy ponders the future of barber poles."

—Charles Kuralt, CBS, *On the Road*

"Garrulous and substantial, Marvy delivers the bluster of P.T. Barnum and the malarkey of the traveling salesman he once was."

—John Margolies, *Gentleman's Quarterly*, December 1984

"Marvy is a substantial, pink-faced man with a sandy mustache and a booming voice...Before meeting Marvy, a visitor imagines someone like the last buffalo hunter, a badlands bad man left over from the century before, gloomily waiting for the great herds to come again. But Marvy sees himself as a man of modern commerce...a kind of spring-wound relic: the breezy, bet-on-the-future confidence of a Midwestern traveling salesman from a half-century ago."

—John Skow, *Time* (magazine), April 21, 1980

"William Marvy looks exactly like the nation's last barber pole manufacturer should look—balding, clipped mustache, half-moon glasses perched halfway down his nose, a cigar clamped in the right corner of his mouth."

—John Camp (who went on to write popular mysteries as John Sanford),
—*St. Paul Pioneer Press*, May 12, 1980

"He sees himself as a man doing his part to keep the barber symbol alive now that other trade symbols—the mortar and pestle for the pharmacist, the three gold balls of the pawn broker, the wooden Indian of the tobacco store—are vanishing."

—Steve Berg, *Minneapolis Tribune*, 1977.

"In the coffee room, where an occasional game of nickel-ante poker is played at lunchtime, Marvy packs his pipe, settles his substantial self into a chair, sets aside his half-moon spectacles, props his wingtips up on a chair. He's ready to talk about the good old days—the days before the Beatles made 'crewcut' a nasty word, when a haircut was a haircut and a shave was a shave."

—Gretchen Legler, *Twin Cities* (magazine), 1985

"He got up from his desk and went into the showroom of the converted car repair shop that has been home to his company...There, high on the wall, resplendent with gold plated castings, was number 50,000.

"'Think of any number between 1 and 68,000,' he said, 'and I'll tell you where those two poles went.'

"'Really?'

"'Do it.'

"'OK; 125 and 62,069.'

"'Come on back to the office.'

"He pulled out two ledger books, one yellowed with age, the other fairly new.

"'No. 125 went to Shakopee, Minnesota, in March 1950 and No. 62,069 went to Burnsby, British Columbia, December 16, 1976.'

"Marvy pointed with his cigar for emphasis.

"'See,' he said."

—Charles Leroux, *Chicago Tribune*, June 25, 1981

FROM PYRAMIDS TO MARVY

A Barbering Timeline

20,000 years ago: Archaeologists have unearthed shaving instruments, razor-sharp grooming flints and clamshell tweezers from the late Stone Age Neolithic period.

biblical times: Genesis 41:14: "When Joseph was summoned to meet the Pharaoh, a barber was sent for to shave him, so that the Pharaoh would not be offended by a dirty face"; Ezekiel 5:1: "And you, son of man, take a sharp knife, take a barber's razor, and cause it to pass upon your head and upon your beard: then take balances to weigh and divide the hair."

4000 BC: Egyptian pyramids include grooming tools and hieroglyphics showing how they were used.

500 BC: Wandering barbers in Greece establish permanent spots where poets, politicians and philosophers would gather and the men of Athens would have their beards trimmed, curled and perfumed. Greek barbers also set broken bones, gave enemas and used bloodletting to try to cure the ailing.

350 BC: The Greeks, under Alexander the Great, lose battles with the Persians, who grabbed their beards. Alexander commands his troops to shave.

300 BC: Romans use the term *barbatulus* and *barbatus* for bearded, unshaved barbarians—stemming from the Latin *barba* (beard), from which "barber" is derived. They devise their own razor around 296 to improve sanitation. All free men of Rome were clean shaven while slaves wore beards.

AD 400: Warring bearded barbarians from the north and west of Europe invade the Roman Empire and carry back Greco-Roman traditions of barbering: wound dressing, bloodletting, bone-setting and teeth pulling.

1100: Longhaired men are barred from Catholic churches, and when they die, others are not allowed to pray for them. The first recorded barber union appears in France, where the archbishop of Rouen bans beards.

1163: Pope Alexander III prohibits clergymen from performing bloodletting, something monks had done for centuries to treat everything from sore throats to the plague. Barbers, adept at working with sharp tools, pick up the slack.

1252: An official barber organization is formed in France, and barbers routinely served as surgeons, performing bloodletting to purge disease, teeth pulling and grooming. Leeches were often used to draw blood believed to carry disease.

1450: English Parliament incorporates the Guild of Surgeons with the Barbers' Company, passing an act that restricts barbers to bloodletting, tooth-pulling and regular tonsorial duties and "forbidding barbers from taking under their care any sick person in danger of death."

1530: Ambroise Paré, considered the father of modern surgery, gets his start as a barber-surgeon.

1541: King Henry VIII grants a combined Company of Barbers-Surgeons.

1745: King George II formerly splits the barbers and surgeons, leaving many barbers to become wig makers.

1850: The American beard comes into its own during the Civil War, and barbers work alongside blacksmiths and candle makers. But slaves and servants start cutting their wealthy owners' hair and beards, and the barbers' prestige sinks.

1880: About forty-five thousand U.S. barbers are serving a population of fifty million. A century later, there would be about twice as many barbers serving a country whose population had increased fivefold.

1886: At the convention that formed the American Federation of Labor, the Journeymen Barbers' Protective Union is represented.

1897: The first barber licensing law is passed in Minnesota. Other states follow, setting up minimum ages, exams and inspections.

1903: Mair (also spelled Mayer) Mairovitz emigrates from Latvia to New York. Ellis Island records show four Mairovitzes arriving on ships between 1900 and 1903, but it's unclear if this is the carpenter whose fear of heights would prompt him to move to Minnesota and smaller buildings.

November 25, 1909: William Mairovitz, Mair and Molly's fifth of six children, is born at home on Smith Avenue in St. Paul.

1913: A St. Louis barber still offers leeching as a service.

1918: William Marvy, age nine, remembers selling newspapers on Armistice Day, ending World War I.

1920s: Most barber poles are painted columns of wood or wind-up models that will swirl for twelve hours if the barber remembers to wind them in the morning.

1922–35: Marvy starts as an errand boy mailing circulars for a barber supply firm in St. Paul, where his sister works as a bookkeeper. He climbs the ranks to salesman, supplying barbershops across southwestern Minnesota with clippers, tonics and barber poles.

1930: American painter Edward Hopper makes a stand-up pillar barber pole the focal point of his masterpiece *Early Sunday Morning.*

1935: William Mairovitz and many relatives go to the Ramsey County Courthouse and have their names legally changed to Marvy in the hope of avoiding anti-Semitic treatment.

1936: After working for two barber supply employers, Western and Empire, that went broke during the Depression, Marvy strikes out on his own, forming the William Marvy Company.

November 25, 1938: Marvy proposes to Rose Goldberg on Thanksgiving and his birthday. Rose was born the same day as he was, and they get married the next year, on January 29.

1946: William and Rose's first child, Edward, dies of sudden pneumonia at age five.

1948: Robert Marvy is born. He will one day replace his father as the company's leader.

1949: The number of U.S. barbers sits at a robust ninety-two thousand, and William Marvy and his engineer friend and neighbor, Bill Harris, tinker with a modern barber pole prototype in the Marvy basement.

January 1, 1950: Marvy and Harris plug in their new, rustproof, shatterproof, lightweight Marvy Model 55 prototype, and Marvy's sons, Bob and Jim, flip the switch.

1953: Mair Mairovitz, William's father, dies at seventy-nine. His tombstone, in English and Hebrew, said he was a devoted husband and father.

1955: The William Marvy Company sells its 10,000th pole.

1961: With business booming, the William Marvy Company leaves its three storefronts in downtown St. Paul and moves into its current home—a former bakery warehouse and auto garage—on St. Clair Avenue just east of Snelling Avenue.

1964: The Beatles with their mop-top haircuts, invade the United States, appearing on the *Ed Sullivan Show*.

1967: Hippies stage the first "Human Be-In" in San Francisco, and long hair becomes a symbol of anti–Vietnam War sentiment. The William Marvy Company cranks out its 50,000th barber pole that same year and manufactures a company-record of 5,100 barber poles. The 112,000 U.S. barbershops in existence will dwindle by two-thirds within the next thirty years.

January 30, 1974: CBS's Charles Kuralt airs his visit with William Marvy on his *On the Road* series.

1980: Marvy barber pole sales dip to an all-time low of fewer than four hundred.

1982: William Marvy is inducted into the National Barber Hall of Fame in Ohio despite having never cut a lock of hair.

March 23, 1993: William Marvy dies at eighty-three.

May 5, 1998: The 75,000th Marvy barber pole is accepted into the Smithsonian Institution's National Museum of American History.

2014: The William Marvy Company fills orders for 598 barber poles, a slight uptick in sales with roughly one-third heading for decorative use in dens or antique settings.

BIBLIOGRAPHY

BOOKS

Barlow, Ronald. *The Vanishing American Barbershop*. St. Paul, MN: William Marvy Company, 1996.

DePaola, Joseph, and Milton Lee. *The Ancient and Honorable Barber Profession*. Chicago: Journeymen Barbers, Hairdressers, Cosmetologists and Proprietors International Union of America, AFL-CIO, 1968.

Hunter, Mic. *The American Barbershop: A Closer Look at a Disappearing Place*. Mount Horeb, WI: Face to Face Books, 1996.

Katz, Donald. *Home Fires: An Intimate Portrait of One Middle-Class Family in Postwar America*. New York: HarperCollins, 1992.

Mills, Quincy T. *Cutting Along the Color Line: Black Barbers and Barbershops in America*. Philadelphia: University of Pennsylvania Press, 2013.

Ringsak, Russ, and Denise Remick. *Minnesota Curiosities: Quirky Characters, Roadside Oddities & Other Offbeat Stuff*. Guilford, CT: Morris Book Publishing LLC, 2003.

ARTICLES AND RADIO SCRIPT

Attoun, Marti. "William Marvy Barber Poles." americanprofile.com, January 16, 2013.

Berg, Steve. "He's Waging One-Man War to Save the Barber Pole." *Minneapolis Tribune,* January 27, 1977.

Boardman, Lawrence. "St. Paulite Invents Different Barber Pole." *St. Paul Sunday Pioneer Press*, May 31, 1953.

Brown, Curt. "For Barber Poles, Turn to the Marvys; a Family Business in St. Paul Keeps an Age-Old Tradition Alive." *Minneapolis Star Tribune,* June 26, 1997.

Camp, John. "Barber Pole Business Goes Around and Around." *St. Paul Pioneer Press*, May 12, 1980.

Downs, Ed. "The Ultimate Barber Pole Maker." *Northliner Magazine*, March 1, 1977.

Eberlein, Cathy. Unpublished TV-radio script, 1979.

Kuralt, Charles. *On the Road*. CBS, January 30, 1974.

Legler, Gretchen. "Stripes Forever." *Twin Cities* magazine, January 1985.

Leroux, Charles. "A Survivor with Style: The Barber Pole King." *Chicago Tribune,* June 25, 1981.

Margolies, John. "The Last Barber Pole Factory." *Gentleman's Quarterly*, December 1984.

Martin, Douglas. "The Smithsonian Celebrates Barbicide." *New York Times*, June 22, 1997.

Marvy, Scott. (1989). Unpublished Sibley High School project in which he recorded and transcribed an interview with his grandfather four years prior to William Marvy's death.

McCabe, Robert. "No You're Not Tipsy: That One Barber Pole Just Looks Like Three; Suppliers Boom New Model as First 'Improvement' in Old Emblem in 25 Years." *Wall Street Journal*, August 21, 1952.

McEachern, Maragaret. Unpublished freelance article, 1972.

Moench-Kelly, Shelley. "This Year Marks the 75th Anniversary of the William Marvy Co…" *Beauty Store Business* magazine, 2011.

Rosenkrantz, Linda. "Barbershop Harmonies." *Renninger's Antique Guide*, March 4–17, 1991.

Skow, John. "In Minnesota, Poles and Profits." *Time*, April 21, 1980.

Sorenson, Sue. "The Last of Its Kind." *Corporate Report*, December 1980.

Smithsonian National Museum of American History news release. "The Smithsonian Accepts 75,000[th] Barber Pole." February 1, 1998.

Woltman, Nick. "St. Paul Company Has the Exclusive on the Barber Pole, an Age-Old Symbol of the Craft." *St. Paul Pioneer Press,* June 22, 2013.

WEBSITES AND LINKS

Antique Barber Chairs Online. www.antiquebarberchairs.net.

Auctions America. http://tinyurl.com/lnz6a39.

Bowman Beauty & Barber Supply. www.bowmanbeauty.com.

"Cutting Along the Color Line: Black Barbers and Barber Shops in America." University of Pennsylvania Press. www.upenn.edu/pennpress/book/15150.html.

Family Business Institute. familybusinessinstit.reachlocal.com.

"History of Barbers." Thames Salon Online. http://www.thamessalon.com/site/barberhistory.htm.

"A History of the African-American Barbershop." Marketplace: Economy. www.marketplace.org/topics/economy/history-african-american-barbershop.

The National Barber Museum and Hall of Fame. www.nationalbarbermuseum.org.

"Shave and a Haircut $60,000! 1969 Barber Shop Car by Joe Bailon Lot No. 2004." Video. http://tinyurl.com/q99tr7f.

"Why Are Barber Poles Red, White and Blue?" Ask History. History.com. www.history.com/news/ask-history/why-are-barber-poles-red-white-and-blue.

William Marvy Company official website. www.wmmarvyco.com.

Index

About the Author

C urt Brown earned degrees in history and American studies from Macalester College, around the corner from the William Marvy Company in St. Paul, Minnesota. He has worked for the *Fergus Falls (Minnesota) Daily Journal*, the Associated Press and the *St. Paul Pioneer Press* and spent twenty-six years at the *Minneapolis Star Tribune*. His 2008 book, *So Terrible a Storm* (Voyageur Press), chronicled a nasty 1905 gale that prompted the construction on Split Rock Lighthouse. He was named Minnesota Journalist of the Year by the Society of Professional Journalists for his 2012 series and e-book *In the Footsteps of Little Crow*, which told the story behind the U.S.-Dakota War. He also earned journalism honors for his coverage of

Photo by John Doman.

the North Dakota oil boom, the 10th anniversary of the 9/11 terror attacks and the 150th anniversary of Gettysburg as told through the eyes of George Buckman, a carpenter-turned-soldier and medic from Minnesota. He lives with his wife, Adele, outside Durango, Colorado.

Visit us at
www.historypress.net
....
This title is also available as an e-book